MONEY
what's left what's right

By the
Accidental Millionaire

DHANASHREE BHATKAL

INDIA • SINGAPORE • MALAYSIA

ISBN 979-8-88733-689-3

for Mom,

My First & Biggest Fan!

Contents

3. Financial Freedom Plan ~ What's Left

4. Conclusion

Acknowledgements

This Book, and many aspects of my Life would remain unfinished if some of the strongest influences who have entered both, are not mentioned. There is no chronology in terms of time, nor in importance of the order in which I mention people!

With *Immense Gratitude* I would like to Thank my Spiritual Master, Gurudev Sri Sri Ravi Shankarji. With whom I found the culmination of my Spiritual journey (that I didn't even know I was on)!

My Mom, Asha Anil Bhatkal, to whom I dedicate this Book. My first Fan, My Role Model, from whom I learnt almost every skill I have. My Shock Absorber and the most Powerful Manifester I know, who remains the biggest reason for me being an Accidental Millionaire! Thank You Mom for always reminding me that 'I am Enough'!

Suman Makhija, My Co-Founder at A Money Tree, the one who was instrumental in introducing me to my Spiritual Journey, and from whom I have learnt the most invaluable Lessons on Business, Entrepreneurship and the Abundance Money Mindset! My Partner in Dime, Crime and Rhyme. Thank You Suman, for being on this Journey with me, for being the one to bring me from Accident to Intention!

Neha, not born to my parents but who has been more than a sibling. Especially in the last three grueling years of my life, in this phase of transformation and re-building. Thank You Neha, for stepping into mom's shoes in every way you could, although we both know they are large shoes to fill!

My Dad, Anil Mangesh Bhatkal, I have his forehead people say. I have his IQ mom said. Ideologically poles apart & with our share of Differences. Yet he has been instrumental in my tryst with Money! Thank You Dad.

Thank You to everyone who has been a part of my journey, during the making of this Book and of my Life.

Several out of them appear in anecdotes, narrations or in silent recollections in the book.

Disclaimer

The information provided in this book is for educational purposes only. It is not intended to be a source of financial or legal advice. Making adjustments to a financial strategy or plan should only be undertaken after consulting with a professional. The publisher and the author make no guarantee of financial results obtained by using this book.

Neither the publisher nor the author shall be held liable or responsible for any loss or damage allegedly arising from any suggestion or information contained in this book.

Connect with Me

Instagram & Facebook:

@dhanashreebhatkal I @amoneytreeonline I @godluvsfun

www.dhanashreebhatkal.com

1.
Introduction

Chapter 1.0
Is This Book for You?

This book is most certainly for you if money alludes you. If you often feel you are at 99, missing that last winning stroke, or if you still find yourself lost when everyone around you seems to be making sense of their lives, this book might help you to dip into your own life to find some answers.

This is not an attempt to follow any principles of attraction by disproving that a component of what happens is attributed to luck or fate by whatever name it is called. Fate does play a role; so does the inner work we do to keep our frequency high, continue to do good work, work on our spiritual side and finally, do everything within our reach to make informed decisions, plan for our future and work towards our goals.

This book works on two controllable factors among these three. The Inner Work and the Practical Work to Set Goals and Achieve them is what we call transformational work.

If money and success have been elusive for you, if relationships are not very supportive either, this book might help you to delve into looking at where the effort has to be made inside of you, when you work really hard on the outside. Believe me; sometimes, the tweaks we need within ourselves are so small that it is unfathomable when we start this dialogue at first. It's unfathomable that this pin-sized thing could keep you small and block your own growth.

If you live paycheck to paycheck, this one is surely for you. There are no quick-fix formulae and nothing that can work like a plug-and-play model. But there are ideas, experience sharing and anecdotes and stories of people who were where you are and crossed over to where they wanted to be. It comes from the premise that all transformation and progress happen inside out.

The reason why the first part of the book, which is more abstract, is the real work is that I believe we must all do and continue to do this to make full use of the second half.

This book is for anyone who loves books and reads to assimilate and collate information. Of course, I don't call it knowledge, because knowledge is a perceived part of information and everyone defines it differently. So, if you are a sucker for books and like to consume anything that might leave you some feel-good tips, this book is most certainly for you.

This might also be for you if you have experienced a sense of "something is amiss" ever in life. On days if you feel you have everything and still seem to find something missing and you can't quite put your finger on it. Maybe, the chapters take you through some of the deep old memories that you don't even know still reside somewhere and cleanse some part of those for you to see things more clearly.

Maybe, it gives you those quick tips to set better and easier goals, given your skills, and not what everyone is getting rich and successful with. If you are already rich and successful and still don't feel fulfilled, you might just find out why.

This book is not for those who have ***Complete Financial Freedom***. If you are fulfilled and have everything you have ever desired, if you truly are living your dream life, then this is certainly not for you. We can connect to co-author the next one since I too am not in that perfectly sorted space yet!

What is This Book About?

This book is a *practical journal* of several things. It comes out of the premise that true *success* and *wealth* mean different things to different people. As we progress through the chapters in this together, we will realize how different our definitions can be. How a balance of every kind of wealth in our lives might be the pathway to real financial freedom and how money really has little to do with financial freedom.

And then, why do success, relationships and health find mention in this book at all? Have you heard the old adage, "Money can't buy everything?" That is only partly true! Even if that is not a politically correct statement to make, you will find several times in the book that I am rarely politically correct!

Well, money can buy the means to get everything. It can't buy happiness, but it can buy you a home, a car, and a bank balance that can provide for life and keep you stress-free. It can buy you gym memberships and nutritionists who can help you create enhanced health. It can also help you to build a happier, less stressful life with the one you love and substantially reduce the chances of a conflict. Money can indirectly buy a lot of things. So, like every other resource, money is not the end but is an extremely important means to an end.

And that end is happiness. Feeling good. Feeling accomplished, confident and high energy. Getting out of bed every morning, feeling excited to be living. And how each of us defines that may differ, but the essence is always the bliss/happiness/fulfilment [by whatever name called] that everyone is looking for.

Why Should I Be Writing This?

I have had a journey from accident to intention. I have seen a sharp rise in wealth in my life while finding extremely good relationships and self-awareness. I have been fortunate and have done little for any of this to happen until very recently. My dad did one part, and my mom the other.

Their combined mindset and their hard and smart work made them millionaires in a span of ten years. And me? An Accidental Millionaire™!

Having got it easy and in an attempt to fill large shoes, I probably spread myself so thin that I had not much of my own individuality and identity left. Let's say despite being a person who is aware, I was on a path, chasing a dream that wasn't my own. But on many levels, life was a breeze. I don't have a rags-to-riches story; my story is different.

But that comes with its own set of challenges. My journey is about the presumptions people make when they see things come to you too easy, how the world thinks you might have no problems and how overwhelming all that money and success can become if you are someone who wanted to do it all on your own.

My journey from accident to intention is also my journey in bringing about the tweaks. In observing and learning. And a lot of un-learning along the way too. Un-learning the habit of taking money lightly and not having a great relationship with it, in taking it for granted.

My story is about having it all but not utilizing it or taking charge of it in a bid to make it on my own, of giving my power away.

There may be anecdotes and incidents from my own life, and in that sense, it is autobiographical. But it is not about me. It is about the millions of people around the world who pass their lives in a jiffy to look back and find there were so many things they could have learnt earlier – those who live their lives never getting introduced to their superpower. Those who spend their lives chasing a direction where the goal post keeps moving ahead whenever they are almost there. This is the story of the millions of people across the globe who let life pass them by, who have just a little work to do inside to create a huge change outside. But they never get down to doing it or even acknowledging it. It is our story and it is also our way to process, come to terms with, unlearn, upskill and move our life up a notch. Because it is never too late. No matter what age you are, no matter what stage of life you are at, you can start now. You can create magic starting now.

I had a catalyst year in my life 3 years ago, losing out on two very beautiful parts of my life that became the beginning of an inner transformation for me. This book is my attempt to share what I assimilated over the years, some unknowingly. Eschewed, processed and channelized in the last 3 years to build a change in my life and my world. It is my effort to put in a nutshell the first-hand lessons life gave me and what I made of it.

The book is full of worksheets and processes that you can run on your own. These are only to nudge you to think, introspect and find answers you might have been looking away from. Every time you repeat, review or work on these, you might find different answers, and newer facts might come up.

The time and energy you give to these - the work you do will determine how much you can take from these and imbibe into your daily life. You might like to make notes, review them often and come back to the processes whenever you feel you need to get further rooted in them.

Let it stay with you as and when possible, and let it be absorbed deeper as it starts to become a habit.

Chapter 1.1

How to Use This Book

This book could be your guide or a series of worksheets you use repeatedly to unearth things about yourself and to increase productivity to reach your *Dream Life*.

But I would best describe it to be your companion. Like the subtle monsoon sky, where the familiar scent lingers long after… Like a constant reminder and catalyst to create change and a complete transformation in how you experience and deal with money.

This book is full of anecdotes of stories from my own life and of others. It puts together decades of reading on the subject, coaches I have worked with and everything money, which has been my central subject.

I am an intentional entrepreneur. I wanted to be one since school and I prepared for it while I finished my post graduation and professional education. I became an entrepreneur and started my own corporation with a concept that was unique to India at that time. I got a lot of press coverage, and soon, people began to think we were the next big thing!

The following year, the business tanked. The bureaucracy and the red tape in India required plenty of permissions annually, which required more networking than doing the right thing. For a new, out-of-college team, that pressure was too much. Half of my original team had fallen apart by this time.

The next few months and the following bounce back taught me the two biggest lessons of entrepreneurship: teamwork and agility.

We restructured our business, changed the way we managed the product and got into the B2B space. We thrived and created a complete turnaround in 5 years. My co-founder, who features silently in this book by being my partner in dime, crime and rhyme, and I, went on to grow the same business [albeit with a different model] to a point beyond our initial expectations.

From a food-focused business in 2002 to Business Transformation Experts in 2010, the journey from surviving to thriving was a long, adventurous and interesting one!

Agility, upskilling, smart work, great goals, leadership, delegation and above all, a great money mindset – to me, this is it in a nutshell!

Rejection and failure bring far more in our professional and personal lives than we can recognise when it is happening. But in hindsight, you will clearly see that every failure prods you forward; every rejection takes you a step closer to new opportunities. What you make of these and how determined you can stay along the path is one of the deciding key factors to what you will eventually become.

Finding a great team can transform your life like nothing else. A great team knows how to put the interest of the unit before themselves and yet, continue to work on individual growth and progress too. Teams that are weak even when individuals in them may be great solo players usually disintegrate. To find people that are aligned to your vision while you are aligned to theirs and to find a way to be agile together and debate when it's required is the best kind of leadership a business can have. The same applies to homes too, where leadership paradigms between the decision makers determine the Happiness Quotient!

In the process of the long winding road from the initial business planning to what it kept emerging and re-inventing itself into, year-on-year, the leadership paradigms kept changing. I believe everyone who was ever a part of the team and leadership did the best they could or knew how to. But when it is time for them to go, it is time to let them go. Eventually, the team that formed and stayed is the current leadership at the firm we founded in 2010. This team was brought about by accident (as I say, a lot of good things in my life have been wonderful, happy accidents!) But during this vigorous process of rejection and redirection, as we learnt the way on our own, I learnt the power of intention. My move from accident to intention has been because of this partnership of 20 years.

We had no mentors; we had to mentor ourselves and sometimes, each other, but having a mentor can make the path much lighter. If you get stuck along the way, I leave enough ways to connect with us. If it works for you, continue with the work in the long haul, and each time you read it or do a process, you will find a new lesson there. That's a promise.

The best way to take everything you can from this book would be to read the chapter and take the worksheets. Practice the techniques provided at the end of the chapter. When you move to the next one, if it is after a gap, read, at least, a part of the previous one to get into the flow. It is not necessary to go through everything in sequence. But if I were you, I would work on the first part of the book before beginning the second.

Financial Freedom to me is, to be able to Generate, Manage and Retain money, and utilise it in the most optimal way to lead a Healthy, Joyous and Happy life.

Money metabolism is two things. For one, it is how much goodness and value you can create in your life with every unit of money you spend. Second, it is the unit of your time and energy that you expend in order to generate each unit of money.

I am wishing you the transformation you want to create in your life! Transformation can be painful sometimes; it can create emotions you didn't know you could feel, sometimes negative. It can bring up memories and stories, and unearth beliefs that you didn't earlier see as separate from you. It might lead to inner conflict or questions. But the outcome is always beautiful.

It could be the gateway to your *dream life*!

A thought to leave you with before you get on this ride – ***Money can buy [almost] Everything!***

Chapter 1.2
Understanding Money

"You must get Control of your Money, or the lack of it will forever Control You."

– Dave Ramsey

Money needs no introduction. We might all have different opinions about it and different relationships with it too. But most certainly, we all want it in varying degrees to fulfil a variety of dreams.

Money is a resource that can create ease in every aspect of life. And yet, what is a basic necessity borders on being a faraway dream. For many, perhaps, three-fourths of the world population, money remains just a dream to chase rather than a reality to enjoy.

The opportunities are aplenty. But financial education has never been a subject in mainstream education. Social media and advertising, in recent years, put the thrust on schemes and various investments with not much explanation behind them. Getting personal advisors is not an affordable option.

In the most simplified format, this is the reason why the rich get richer and the poor get poorer – lack of financial education, no access to correct advice and not being able to dip into the right opportunity.

Money can forever elude you or can be your best friend depending on how you build your relationship with it. This book is built around a simple format to create a relationship with money, invite it into your life and get it to stay. There are two aspects that I have worked with, and this book is a culmination of everything I have learnt, practised and trained people to work with.

The mindset work, the first part, which is in Section 2. Where we work through a step-by-step approach to delve into our memories and stories around money, release our emotions, understand where we are coming from when it comes to money and work on creating the mindset required to recognise and receive it when money knocks on the door.

The second half, Section 3, is the practical approach of how to set your goals, the framework you might need, understand the ideologies you want to work within, deal with rejection and failure, and finally, build your own personalized Money Management System.

Before we begin any of the real work, it would be nice for you to begin with running a quick check on where you are with your money relationship at the moment.

This gives you a starting point to understand the money problems you have. Understand here that *"money problems" don't necessarily mean having less or no money.* Money problems can be of all types. The grass is always green on the other side. It's time to stop looking at the other side of the fence and to start watering the grass on your side!

Evaluate Your Relationship With Money

What does money mean to you? How best would you describe your relationship with it?

Does it support you when you need it? Does money make you feel good and excited about waking up each morning, or does it make you feel like you always have to chase it in order to get its attention?

If you are not a very visual person and can't run this analogy with the abstract concept of money, we can run a few quick questions to get these answers:

1. What is the primary emotion you feel when you think of Money?
2. Do you believe Money always comes to you before or when you need it?
3. Does making Money come easily to you or does it always make you work hard?
4. When you receive Money, do you land up spending it all to zero or always keep aside a saving?
5. Are you in Debt? Loans, Over Drafts, Mortgage on Assets, Credit Cards, Personal Borrowings.
6. Do you have Liquidity if you were to need Money today for an Emergency?

As you run through these questions, you already have an indication of whether money is a problem or you truly have ease with it.

For many who have ease with money too, there is always scope for that small improvement here and there that can put some more things on track. In fact, if you have ease with receiving money, you already have an advantage. By the end of this book, you probably can create a plan that you can execute much faster.

Managing Money

Managing money is far more difficult than earning it. Traditional ways of life teach us methods to earn, but rarely are we taught by the system as to how we could manage our money better to create powerful income-expenditure-savings buckets in our life. What ensues then for most is a battle between earnings, increasing costs, the desire to upgrade lifestyle and the need to save. The balance is not created by accident. The balance can only be brought about by a concerted effort to understand the paradigms of money, and then, use them to our advantage.

Why Do Most Businesses Fail in the First Three Years?

Do you know less than 3% of businesses actually survive for more than 10 years? Do you know a whopping 75% fail in the first 3 years and another 12% over the first 5?

Although the reasons for any failure are always multiple and can never be attributed to any one thing, one of the most common recorded reasons statistically is the lack of money management skills. Most businesses have a learning curve of 12-18 months, during which they need to remain agile and implement their newly acquired lessons quickly.

When money management skills are lacking, leaders often try to fill the gaps with an infusion of new funds. The pressure on liquidity and gaps in the revenue cost creates panic and repeated fund infusion starts becoming a cycle, with the hope each time that these inflows will give the business a new league.

But then, money problems are usually not about money. The infused funds do not solve the problem but make the gap wider. Businesses get into a spiral and the inevitable is waiting to happen.

A small tweak and the right methodology to manage money, restructure costs, retrain teams and bring in new financial systems can create a business transformation if done in time. But most business owners keep working on the myth that bringing in more debt or investments will solve the problem until there is nothing left to salvage.

Why Do Individuals Suffer From Money Problems?

Humans are a complicated species. Money as a denominator can add a little zing to that complexity!

Picture this. You want someone in your life. Why? Because they can bring you comfort, luxury and even power. So, you chase that someone, on one hand, doing all you can, working "hard" and doing everything that you have heard works. And then, you are judgemental about them. You ridicule them at times. Do you think you would be able to attract them into your life if your true feelings are mixed? Do you think you can do your

100% if you have mixed emotions coming up about them?

Money brings up emotions, those we can't put a finger on. Maybe, you have been embarrassed about having too little or about having too much. Maybe, you feel guilty about having that fancy trip to come back home and meet a close friend who shares that he is having trouble making both ends meet. Maybe, you just got an appraisal and found out the same day that your sibling was fired from their job. Maybe, you lost a parent when you were a child, and every time you have a jackpot win or a bumper amount, you feel a sense of loss all over again, almost guilty that they weren't able to enjoy what you are enjoying now. Maybe, you had a difficult childhood and saw your family having to work really hard for money. And so, now if it comes to you easy, maybe with a speaking gig or with a short stint of work you actually enjoy, you feel guilty for having it easy when your family had it difficult.

Wanting to do something and not having money to do it is the smallest of the money problems because it is visible. Not being able to afford something is in the face. You see it so you are aware of the problem even if you don't have the solution yet. But some money problems are far deeper. Identifying them might have to be the first step to even knowing they exist. And only then can you plan how you would resolve them.

Introduction to Financial Freedom

Financial Freedom is a state where you can earn, manage and retain all the money you want to maintain the lifestyle you want, be with the people you want, have great health and find fulfilment, where money becomes the catalyst to live a complete, fulfilled and happy life.

In the work I do, I often come across people who are chasing numbers in the financial world. They are so feverish about the money they want to make that they often don't have the time to ask themselves a simple question – what do they want to do with all that money!

The value of money is in what it can buy you. And although money might not buy everything, it can certainly make a lot many things easier and more accessible. It is a means and not the end. If you don't know what matters to you and what your life goal is, your financial gains or goals are going to remain just a number. To aim for complete financial freedom, you have to know what matters to you, what you are aspiring for and what is your calling in life. Knowing that makes the entire process easier.

If you are someone who is in their 20s and aims for financial freedom, if you are an avid biker, an artiste and your dream is to travel the world on bike trips, if that is your passion, money is likely your tool to provide for enough to be able to do these trips for life while it covers all your costs. If you have no dependents and already come from a financially well-placed family, the task at hand might be even lighter.

Viz-a-viz, if you are in your 50s, aiming for complete financial freedom, have a family of 6 and have struggled with a business which is failing for years, you have finally come to terms with that but have no idea what to do next. You might be at a point where debt is mounting, healthcare costs are going up since you have senior parents, your kids are growing up and their education will only get more expensive. You are the only earning member and this business was the main source of earnings for the family. The aim and the way to get there might for now look like a far-fetched dream.

Your situation might be a third, as unique as you are. But wherever you are, you can get started today and build the life of your dreams. Understanding the concepts, training yourself to function from a different space, being goal bound, time-bound and holding yourself accountable each day go a long way. Discipline is always the cornerstone of success in whatever you set out to do.

Financial Freedom can be a reality for you; for anyone who seeks it and is willing to give it their 100%. Goal setting and planning always mean starting from wherever you are at. We can't go back and change time. But we can do things differently starting now.

That is where the Magic begins. In the Now.

2.
Money Mindset ~ What's Right

Chapter 2.0
What Was That Dream?

> *"When we are first born, with a clean slate and zero baggage, God whispers a dream into our ears."*

I grew up believing that. I am not sure if this was an early story told to me by someone before I could really understand or remember who did, or if it really was something that just dawned on me. But all my life, I have felt like I was God's special child and that something was whispered to me when I was born.

In hindsight, I have come to realize that it indeed is the case for every one of us. We might call that power God, the Universe, The Divine or simply a superpower. Some of us might not acknowledge or want to call it anything. And we might then, decide to attribute this first whispered dream to any force that we believe in. I shall refer to this force as God for the sake of brevity.

As kids, we often might have had big dreams, and although different for each of us and changing with time, there is something that that initial dream would reveal to you about yourself.

When I was a child, I wanted to be a doctor [that was the longest dream I nurtured], but simultaneously, I wanted to do many different things. Trainer/Teacher, Social

Worker, Business Person, Politician, Freedom Fighter, Pilot. Different years; different things.

I knew it was a changing dream and so did the adults around me. After all, some of my most accomplished family members started out wanting to be bus drivers. But looking back, now I find the common thread. My whispered dream was really about making a difference, touching the lives of people, and being in the driving seat. What I was expressing were ways I thought of getting there. As a child, I didn't know the connection. Perhaps, I didn't know why this range of things showed up as fleeting ambitions in my head. But I can see that in hindsight today.

Of course, I am glad no adult around me spotted that and prodded me on. Like everything else in life, this must be a part of our own self-journey. So, this also means that if you are a parent and are reading this book, please refrain from using the takeaways from it to identify these patterns in your kids. It's their life and let them discover things their own way! For that matter, do not attempt using these for anyone. They are meant for you. When the time is right and they wish to, they will start working on themselves!

Coming back to the dream, can you look back and find the common thread in yours? You can run a quick worksheet at the end of this chapter if you want to prod further and find some interesting bits about yourself.

For most of us, it takes us years to even realize that there was a common thread. So, we give it up, literally write them off like something childish, changing things. "Oh, all kids say that," is a common thing we hear, and we accept it without questions.

For those of us 'others,' we grow up! And life chides us to accept dreams as the more lucrative, more sensible vocational options that the world offers. And instead of looking inside, we start looking at the available opportunities outside and select from them.

The voice that tries to remind us from time to time about how what we do makes us feel, gets silenced with time when bills are waiting at the door. The practical guiding force (read social media) around us tells us how we must be visible, how we must do the cost-benefit analysis for things before we start out and how to best manage our lives and careers.

Our primary instinct, over time, moves to survival and growth, which come from the instinct to survive. Our dreams then, logically, take a back seat or remain unfound for the rest of our lives.

So, when people say follow your heart and passion and that's the way to succeed, does that make the dent? To me, balance has meant everything. And looking back now, I appreciate the importance of balance even more. Your dream, the passion, following your heart is a sure way to find your purpose, to find what it is that will give you fulfilment at the end of your life. Can you think of someone in your life, maybe someone you know directly or even someone you know of, have met over the years even if not closely, who has lived a successful, wealthy and achievement-filled life but has a regret not having done enough?

On the other hand, you would know at least one person who has followed their heart all their life in the bid to achieve their purpose and not used much of the practical side. So to say, the world couldn't touch their dreams in one way. But it's most likely that their sense of fulfilment might be the same as the first category eventually.

The former may have regret or resentment. The latter may have the very same for different reasons. Then, what might be a way, a middle path we can find?

A balance of both – the blend of finding our dream, our common thread and thus, our *life's purpose*. And finding a practical, lucrative path of least resistance to get there.

A balanced life, where we hone our skills, meet the right people, where we work on the inside and outside. Where we challenge what is given down to us by the world, polish our own rough edges and then, get prepared to take life on.

And is there an ideal time to do that? Of course, the earlier the better, because you find fulfilment and the balance faster and earlier. But really, the time is where you are at. In your 20s, 30s 40s, 70s, or 80s, it really doesn't matter. Fulfilment, success and even wealth is a very personal journey. And inside us, we are always the same kids we were when we were 5 years old. The age is on the outside. The time is now. And the magic is you.

Are You Enough?

All our lives, we will meet different kinds of people. There are some who think we are not enough and some who think we are just too much. And rarely will you come across or be fortunate to meet someone who knows and tells you that you are enough. They see your flaws, they can see the areas you might need to work on, and yet, they can see that you are enough. Just right for the purpose you came into this world for. Have you had someone tell you that?

I had my mom. We had a surrounding that was extremely violent and abusive in my formative years. A joint family set up with an uncle so violent that I have had to undergo therapy even as a child to deal with that. The living room often was a battleground for his and his wife's toxic relationship on full display with things hurled at each other from two ends of the room. That there were 8 others living in the same house [two of them their own kids] didn't seem to deter them from what was a pattern for close to 6 years of my daily life. And yet, I was a happy child. A confident child. Of course, I did have a tendency for aggressive behaviour, which is what was being corrected during those therapy sessions, but I was still someone who could make friends easily, relate to people, learn things quickly and connect with myself. I just knew I was enough.

My mom made sure she built a world within that world that was mine. We had a room in that house, and once I was inside, I stepped into my world. It's where my dreams, skills, my thoughts, feelings and conversations mattered. Where mornings began with the *Jack and the Beanstalk* [a fairy tale different from the damsel in distress and prince on a white horse! – Another lesson there.] as the breakfast story. It was followed by school time and then, a routine of my own. In hindsight, I realize that when we were in our room, my mom never discussed what had or was happening outside. We were in our world where everything was good, where I was enough. Where I was God's special child and the world was a beautiful place.

Keeping my sanity and her's in that house – I realize looking back – would have been a mammoth task. Here was a man who would hold me up and hurl me towards the balcony every time he wanted to threaten my mom to say yes to something he wanted done. All of maybe 3 or 4, those jitters stayed in my mind and body for a very long time even after we moved out of there.

But this is not about my uncle or his toxicity. This is about my mom and the beautiful world she gave me. Amidst all that craziness, was a sane space where we read books together; she read out inspiring anecdotes to me and sometimes, I read out books to her too. She made sure I knew and felt I was enough!

Many years later, I would often hear comments like "Oh, your confidence? Obviously, that comes from the money you are sitting on!" For those I met in my teens or after and who came into my life where I was already in that space, it is difficult for them to believe that I would have had the same level of confidence [some call it arrogance] when we were in an extremely toxic environment. But those who knew me at school and in my early life know that my level of confidence has always been this way.

I always felt and believed that life is good and I will always get only the best. That, I can achieve what I want and I can upskill and learn anything that I would ever want to. That, people in general, are good and the world is a fair place. That, we live in a beautiful nation and it's better to make a change than to blame the government. I learnt in my world that books can be my best friends and can teach me so much more than institutions can in a lifetime. I got to learn that education is not about the degree we obtain but what stays with us after we have forgotten everything in the books. That money can't buy *class*. That, transforming the lives of those around us is easier and faster than waiting for one day when we can transform the world. That every day, we have a chance to touch the lives of people with whatever we have and we have to wait for nothing. That, *being rich, being brilliant and being kind are not necessarily mutually exclusive options. You can easily be all three!*

My mom and I journeyed together through many tough times, meandering into areas we had to find our way out of. Which we did. My mom was my first and biggest fan. And if it wasn't for her, I would have given into the ways of this world a long time ago.

Do you have that one person (or more if you are fortunate) who makes you realize you are enough every day? If not, can you be that person to yourself?

Worksheet – Join the DOTS [Finding Your Dream/Purpose]

1. What were the Five [or Ten] Things you wanted to be as a child? List them Out.

   ----

2. Against each of these, describe what about it was fascinating for you then.

   ----

3. Which of the things that fascinated you then fascinate you still? Or hold value for you today?

   ----

4. If you had infinite money, time and energy, what are the three things you would like to do for the rest of your life?

   ----

5. Write down the Three Common Threads you find. [Attributes, Larger Purpose, Fun, Ambition, People, World at Large, Anything]

   ----

6. Is there a way that the Vocation/Profession/Business/Life that you currently lead can connect the dots to this common thread? If yes, then write three things you need to do to actually build that connection. If not, then write three skills you need to work on as a road map to finally join the dots.

From the Support Toolkit

Panchakosha Meditation, unravelling the five sheaths of our being, to reach our inner selves. An ideal place to begin the Meditational journey for beginners and for a quick inner check for stalwarts too.

There are many versions of it. I recommend:

https://youtu.be/6bGlFwNfRGg

Chapter 2.1
Healing Money Memories

"I have come to understand a person's Wounds by the Joy they resist."

– Itiola Jones

Memories are a fascinating thing. While the storage serves us to run our lives more smoothly and efficiently, the same storehouse also has a strange way of saving and throwing up unnecessary information when we expect it the least.

As children, you are exposed to your firsts. Based on what your predominant sensory style is, you could go back in time and relive your memories through the use of that sense. You would remember incidents and events through that predominant sense more easily.

So, if you are a visual person, you have a tendency to visualise whatever you listen to or read about. This is your sensory superpower and you can transport yourself back in time to relive it through visualisation. Your sensory power is vision.

This might be different for people who are more auditory and whose sensory superpower is listening.

Likewise, you could be someone whose sensory superpower is touch [Kinesthetic Learning] and you learn things best by being hands-on, by exploring and feeling and touching.

Nature has left a key with you to go back and relive the memories which can help you cleanse your experience and actually rewire your system. If you have read about past life regression or the use of hypnosis in treating even grave conditions, you already know that releasing stored memories that don't serve us anymore, can bring Magical Transformation in our body, mind and soul.

The purpose of this chapter is to find and locate the memories that don't serve us in any way anymore and let them go. And each time you run the processes that you find here, you will most likely come across something more to let go of. Trust the process. This is not created by me or anyone else. It is a natural way of healing that life has gifted us with.

You can find ways outside of this book also to find and let go of the memories that you need to. Go all out and get the path you want to. Some of the most tried and widely used methods are mentioned in the end. You might want to explore any of these methods too.

But before all this, let's first answer the question in your mind right now.

"How would remembering childhood events and reliving and releasing them help? If I don't remember and have to dig for them, it means they are forgotten, already! Why unearth them now?"

The answer to that lies in the doing of it. If you see money patterns in your life that you can't explain with logic, you can already identify that there are things deeper that you might need to reach and excavate before you clear them out and get ready for bigger better things.

Maybe, you repeatedly get into patterns of debt or your money invariably gets stuck or you just can't ever say 'No' to friends or family and land up foregoing your own plans in order to solve other people's money problems.

Maybe, you are always paying all the bills and taking your car out for group outings and secretly, you even feel resentful of it at times, but it's a habit you can't seem to break.

Maybe, you are on the other side. Always feeling like others have to do things for you and you can never seem to solve your own money problems and that shame or embarrassment is your money problem.

Patterns can point to deeper memories that continue to create the undercurrent and trouble us inside until we become aware of them and finally set them and us free. Since you have started this journey to attain Financial Freedom, we must start where it all began. To set ourselves free first from everything that holds us back. Only then can we take new flight towards what we want to achieve.

Reality Vs Perception

Let's start from your very first memory of money.

What is really the first thing you remember when you were 3 years old?

[Most of us tend to remember things vividly in our subconscious minds from the time we were 2 or 3 years old. If we dig deeper, we can retrieve them easily.]

Maybe, the time you put a coin in your mouth and someone said, "Don't! That money is dirty!"

Or you overheard elders talk about money and how it had changed your friendly neighbour! It can really be that small a thing you are digging for!

Do not pre-decide what memory or age to go back to. More often than not, the memory that resides might be so subtle you don't even know it. Dig deeper, give yourself a few minutes. This is intense work and it is important you find your time and space whenever you can to work on this.

The end of this chapter has a resource you can work with. But before that, do this exercise on your own. There are usually several memories we need to unearth which might not always be retrieved in pre-created work sheets.

How was the situation around you when you were growing up? Remember that your reality might be very different from what the situation really was. As kids, we tend to interpret things very differently from what they might really be.

For example, a friend shares that as a 4-year-old, when her parents separated, she heard a lot of bickering in the house, and most of the conversations were about assets, division and negotiation over what was jointly held between them. This was interpreted by her inner child to mean they did not have enough money, and once their family split, she would have to invariably struggle to get even a "normal" life. Something that further strengthened this was the societal conversations she overheard about her mother having to battle this out alone since she didn't have a strong support system. She lived with this fear and insecurity inside her for the coming decades despite the fact that after the separation, things between the parents remained amicable, both were individually well-placed and she never really had to go through any struggle. She had to do several months of inner work to let that memory [her interpretation of it] go before she recognised that the truth was far different from her version of it.

But, even if the interpretation and the fact are the same, holding on to a memory doesn't serve us in any way.

What is your inner child memory?

Did you grow up feeling poor?

Or rich and embarrassed about it?

Did you often sense that you took too much from those around you? Maybe, there was that rich uncle who always paid the bills and threw lavish parties, when you overheard your parents converse about how they were struggling to make both ends meet?

Or, perhaps, you had parents who spent easily, lent money to friends and family and rarely got it back?

Did you feel guilty about yourself in any form?

A parent telling you that they went through hell to bring you into the world, or they had to struggle too much to keep you safe or they left a better life because you were more important to them? Common things parents and families say to make the child feel important but usually, have the contrary impact!

What did these make you feel? How does it reflect in your life today?

Did you have parents or family who complimented you a lot or not at all?

Before you work on this, please be sure to remind yourself that you fully acknowledge that sharing this story (even with yourself) does not mean you are running down the people you love. Completely understand that our parents did the best they knew how and this dialogue we are having is only to heal ourselves and, perhaps, in a way, them too.

Many of the people we have loved and continue to love might not have got a chance to find healing or techniques to actually deal with their own issues. So, do not get into a space of judgement or guilt. Just do this exercise in a space of finding your own healing to transform your life. Healing family patterns can heal not only us but also our families and end the energetic negative patterns from moving to the next generation.

In many cultures or families, praising one's own children is considered an act of vanity. So, parents tend to undermine their own and sometimes, even amplify the achievements of others.

What was your experience on this?

Did you have parents or family members who often praised you in front of guests and visitors and even to you directly?

When they praised or complimented you, did they also often take credit for it? Or did they leave it to your own skills? A typical customary line you will find often in many societies is for someone to say "oh she/he speaks so well, gets it from..." What did this make you feel?

Or were you never praised or complimented? Did a parent or elder you dealt with a lot have a habit of saying "This is good but you could have done better?" How does that show up for you now? Do you tend to seek validation from others or land up thinking that you are never good enough?

Most often, the parenting principles that people have followed over the last few decades tend to be based on an orthodox mindset carried down from generations and not assessed before applying. What they might intend to inspire us with can leave a by-product in the form of a memory that can leave us confused. Sometimes, it impacts us deeply for life.

I was born to my parents after a series of painful miscarriages. Almost seven. Time and again, I remember this being discussed in the house, sometimes thinking I wasn't listening and at other times, within my earshot. I understand today that they were only sharing their own struggle and how they overcame it.

It was a discussion about victory and glory and how they overcame a hurdle to achieve what they wanted. For them, the story was of a 'Win.' And if spoken in front of me, they spoke in a way to make me feel special. Like the child, they waited for and went through so much to have. But was this the memory I made around it?

Certainly not. For me, it became a mix of very different and opposed feelings.

On one hand, it was a reminder that I was responsible for so many struggles that my family had to go through, emotionally, financially and mentally. And I should have made it easier by not taking this long to arrive [sounds crazy right? But look within and find that crazy memory that resides within, which now looks completely unfounded or even illogical as an adult but which you might be carrying somewhere deep inside!]

On the other hand, it also made me feel a profound sense of obligation. Like they did so much to give me a ticket to this world that I now needed to always feel indebted to them. Even if it meant, at times, that I need to put my own interests second.

I felt important and special, something they wanted to make me feel, but also responsible for everything, even that, which was beyond my control.

It played up in my business and money perspectives in the form of over-delivering on my word, overdoing, or sometimes overstepping to help someone, which might have actually been detrimental rather than empowering, even for them.

When I unearthed these memories, I also found that the embarrassment of having made it so difficult for the family before I was born was so strong that it showed up for me in the form of always going that extra mile to make up for it! I almost felt obliged to everyone around me for bringing me into this world! Unknowingly, I would never say 'No' or take a strong stand for my own feelings or decisions. It led to a secret resentment in every situation where I wanted to do things differently but felt obligated to conform.

This played out in my decisions around the career I chose, the people I dated and even some of the very critical decisions of my life. Until I took charge, did inner work and started afresh.

Do you have a memory from your childhood, which makes you feel like that? Maybe, you understand it better as an adult, but have you processed it really?

Does it make you take up more than is possible at times? Over-deliver, go that extra mile in business or at work even if you know less was enough. Do you tend to always be in an accessible mode because you truly think it is your responsibility? Do you tend to carry the weight of obligation and responsibility too far, and step in to do things for people where sometimes, letting them do it may really be better for both?

Receiving is Key

Money problems are rarely about money. Money memories are rarely about money.

If you can't tell if you are a good receiver or not, ask yourself some of these questions:

Who pays the bill when you go out and it's not discussed prior?

Do you feel guilty to ask someone to split the bill?

Do you offer or even insist to pay?

Do you often drive people home even when it is inconvenient for you and always refuse when someone offers to drop you home?

Do you feel incomplete if you have to use public transport [even uber] since you think it means you are going to have to depend on someone else?

Many of us are great givers. We were taught to share and we grew up believing that not sharing makes us bad people. That's what the fairy tales taught us too. So, we are good with giving away our ideas, our words, our advice, and even gifts and treats.

But when it comes to receiving, it makes us uneasy or even defensive. It can bring about shame or embarrassment based on what our memories are that might be associated with receiving.

In a conversation, when you share something emotional and the listener sympathises with you, do you shrug away or refuse help? When someone gives you a compliment, do you deflect? "Oh, that wasn't really anything much" or "Anyone could have done that" or any instant responses that undermine your win.

Did You Feel You were Judged for Being Yourself?

Some of us are born a bit over-enthusiastic [ask me] and so many of the mortal beings around us fail to understand what keeps our adrenaline so high. This leads to comments, criticism, and sometimes, even being judged as if there was an ulterior motive to it.

In hindsight, I realise that probably it is because most people don't know how to deal with over-enthusiastic people like us. They are used to a certain way how things are done. People are supposed to be quiet and well-behaved, and being enthusiastic should only be when there is something really going on that is worth being exhilarated about. So, if someone appears joyful or just living it up all the time, people are just unsure of how to process that.

I faced this a lot as a child. I would often get asked, "Why can't you sit in a place?" When I grew up, it became, "Why do you have to be so enthusiastic all the time?"

We all have things we got judged for, comments that just fell on our ears. Most often, mine was about being an obstinate child. So, yes, I was dealing with severe abuse inside the house, restricted mostly to the use of our bedroom, only knowing one sane adult [mom] and another who I saw little of [dad] since he was perpetually at work. So, whenever I got a chance to step out, I was free, I was boisterous and also a bit overboard maybe, I have to admit!

I exhibited aggressive behaviour because I had little time to call my own and I wanted to make the most of it. It took me therapy and a lot of effective communication to be able to finally process and overcome that. But a certain level of rebellion and assertion both stayed. Today, when someone says I am intimidating, I take that as a compliment.

As a child, it was offensive, it was hurtful, it was like some adult passing a loose comment and rejecting me for what I was. What do you remember from your childhood that feels like that?

If you don't remember, this is submerged layers beneath. You would remember only when you peel them off. What was the one thing that you didn't like, which adults said about you?

This work can create true freedom. Go back into those memories and write them down in as much detail as you can. Reliving it can be painful. I often find people overwhelmed or feeling the need to cry when they do this. It is a personal process. Do it your way; make it your own.

I suggest you can even take a buddy along once you get comfortable with the process. But the best way is to do it in solitude, in your 'me time' to be able to make the most of it.

All the above examples and instances are only illustrative. Every person will have unique memories that are born out of unique events in their lives. It is unfathomable to cover them all. Many of us might have memories more painful, of abuse, loss or anger or experiences that we choose to keep tucked inside.

If that is something you want to do, it is completely your choice. But there still can be many others you can work on. Every time you do this work, more and newer ones will show up, and as you proceed from time to time to repeat this process, you will find that many of the past memories do not bring about the same intensity of feelings in you anymore.

And remember,

It's never too late to have a happy childhood!

Find Your Sensory Super Power

There are two ways to find this easily:

1. Look out for your own words. Are you more likely to say “look at me” to draw attention to you? Or “Listen to me.” Do you tend to talk more in the likes of see, watch, look or hear, speak, tell? Our lives’ solutions are hidden in clues all around us if we observe them.

2. The other is an easier one. When you recollect a person or have to retrieve it from your memory, what comes to your mind first? The visual or the audio? Do you prefer video meetings to audio calls for important discussions? Do you often think you can “relate” better when you can see rather than only hear someone?

It’s easy to know if your sensory superpower is vision or audio. Use it to dig deeper and find those memories that might be controlling so much of your behaviour without ever coming to the surface. Find the blocks and clear them.

Let’s start making way for your Dream Life!

Worksheet [Forgive and Let Go]

1. List out your money memories [minimum of 20]:
2. Against each memory, write who and what you need to forgive.
3. Forgiveness can be a gentle switch of only being ready. Relive each memory, use your sensory superpower to relive that memory, forgive and let go. Do this individually for each memory. [There is no trick and it is easier said than done. This is why you might need to do this several times before you feel the shift. Just do it and move to the next, to come back to it whenever you feel the need.]
4. Can we find a better experience to replace each of these? [Write down a better perspective to each of the Memory you listed.]
5. Take fresh air or a nap and drink a lot of water after this worksheet is done.

From the Support Toolkit

Indian culture has several ways in which we can release our memories [impressions] through meditation. Yoga is an excellent entry point to get into breath work and meditation. The chapter "Support Toolkit" mentions a complete rhythmic breath work practice that can synergize the system, called the *Sudarshan Kriya.*

Ho'oponopono [Hawaiian Technique of Forgiveness]

This ancient Hawaiian practice of forgiveness functions as both, a communication concept for reconciliation and a tool for restoring self-love and balance.

In practice, it works sort of like a mantra for self-love. And it's super simple.

The word *ho'oponopono* roughly translates to "cause things to move back in balance" or to "make things right." It's a very zen concept. (In native Hawaiian language, "pono" means balance, in the sense of "life." When things are in balance, nothing is *off*, so to speak.)

Accordingly, chanting this prayer over and over is a powerful way to cleanse the body of guilt, shame, haunting memories, ill-will, or bad feelings that keep the mind fixated on negative thoughts.

The ho'oponopono prayer goes like this:

"I'm sorry, I forgive you, thank you, I love you."

That's it. And isn't that something we all need to hear? *"I'm sorry, I forgive you, thank you, I love you."* It's very touching, especially given how simple and universal these words are.

With regular practice, reciting these four simple phrases helps develop self-love and self-esteem at the times when we need it most. In this way, it's both a lullaby to the self and a guaranteed insightful way to approach forgiving other people.

As a forgiveness practice, it is also deeply resonant, as it tends to penetrate our inner monologue over time.

Chapter Summary

- *Identify your Sensory Superpower*
- *Unearth Childhood Memories around how they made you feel about Money*
- *It is never too late to have a Happy Childhood*
- *Forgive and Release*

Chapter 2.2
Releasing Money Emotions

> *"I sat with my Anger for a Long time, until I realised her real name was Grief."*

Every Human being is distinguishable from the rest of the living world for two reasons: the brain and the capacity to process emotions. And most humans, irrespective of their location, gender, age or ethnicity, tend to have emotional baggage in some form or the other. It can range from small irritants to larger unprocessed trauma.

If your instant response to that line is "I have had a good life, I have no trauma," that is the normal response most people have before they start this work.

Understanding how subtle this can be and how it can make its way into our lives is interesting.

Understanding Emotions and How They Impact You

The human tendency to respond to any situation where we perceive risk or threat is to jump into fight or flight mode. An already vulnerable individual often finds it difficult to put up a fight and might resort to escaping reality or the situation that stares them in the face.

The positivity industry has globally made optimism and always wearing the positive mask so popular that underneath this are a range of emotions that people are often forced to hide, in order to fit into the circles around them.

The more known side of people undergoing or having undergone trauma is the visible anxiety, depressive behaviour, substance abuse or even anger and rage issues that can be recognised and treated. The lesser known and undiscussed responses might be the idea of feeling compelled to be happy all the time, thus pushing things under the carpet and not dealing with the reality of what has happened to them.

In both cases, the prominent emotions that emerge obviously under the sheath can be:

Grief, Fear, Guilt, Anger, Shame, Denial, Numbness, Overwhelm, Anxiety, Confusion, Sorrow, Hurt.

Each of these is a powerful emotion and can be channelised positively to overcome the initial response and create a new story too. But the failure to do that, or not getting the right help at the right time can sometimes put people into a spiral of undealt emotions for decades, grappling with the half reality of their existence and never realising their full potential.

A third to the list of flight or fight is freeze. A situation where a person neither escapes nor fights back, but goes numb, hiding behind a different emotion.

We lost an extended family member when I was 7. For most, he was only an uncle. When I carried this trauma to my adulthood, many of my friends couldn't understand why it had to mean so much since it wasn't a parent after all. It is strange how we humans have learnt to compartmentalise even something like grief and trauma as if they come in prescribed formats. Emotions come in many formats and are a mix of so many layers of our existence that no logic really can explain why different people are impacted by the same event in a different way.

The way there are people in the world who can deal with the death of a partner or a parent or even a child, much better than others. There may be many who can't get over the death of a pet for decades. It can be the circumstances, the importance of the person in their lives, what emotional support the event takes away from them and more.

My mama's (maternal uncle's) passing was too many things rolled into one for me. He was not a parent, but he was someone who protected us. During my formative years, whenever I faced emotional violence and abuse in my "home," my mom would take me to my uncle's. That was my safe haven. Somewhere, I knew I was safe. I knew my mother was safe. It was my go-to place and he was my go-to person.

A doctor by profession and a musician by passion, he devoted a lot of his time to family. Pursuing varied, interesting hobbies, he even got onto the society committee and chaired it to spearhead a redevelopment project which was his brainchild. It was during the times when "redevelopment" was not a word that was even discussed in middle-class homes!

He was also a larger-than-life figure for me – someone I believed was a hero, and so, he couldn't die. He wasn't supposed to die because heroes overcome every hurdle. At 7, I thought that applied to death too.

Further adding to the trauma of that night when he passed away was, a distant relative, who for some reason only she knows, locked me up inside the bathroom so that I don't get too near him. "Children shouldn't see all this," was her explanation. For the next 2 hours, no family member realised I was locked up in that chaos. I was let out 2 hours later by someone who heard me. For the two hours, I didn't scream or shout or bang on the door too loudly because I wasn't sure if that was okay to do given my uncle was still there outside.

Years later, even today, I am extremely anxious driving through tunnels during inter-city drives. Much later, when I went for therapy, I discovered that this anxiety had to do with my ordeal that night.

Do you have a memory or story from your list that provokes a strong intense emotion inside, even if the event that triggered it has faded?

When Unprocessed Emotions Can Turn into Trauma

Most of us, actually every one of us, has undergone some kind of trauma to some degree in our lives. We most likely process it as a natural way of moving on in life. The loss of a loved one, personal emotional abuse, our inner dialogues, ill health, and financial misfortunes there can be so many things that leave scars on our minds.

Our society trains us to not look at or talk about our trauma. Mental disturbances of any kind are mostly taboo to talk about in most societies leading to the largest pandemic this world will ever see; "unprocessed trauma" leading to anxiety, depression, and in acute cases, even breakdowns.

Trauma and its impact are not always full-blown. Sometimes, they can be as subtle as a trickle of water that steadily flows underneath. It can go unnoticed for years before the impact really starts showing up in the body or mind.

There can most often be the primary trauma - something that happens directly to a person. Break ups, abuse, ill health, disability, chronic conditions, financial losses, divorce, custody issues, physical attributes, it can be anything which is direct to a person and they experience it themselves.

Secondary or acquired trauma is the more subtle form. Here, the person experiencing the trauma doesn't even realise it themselves. Neither do they receive support from their surroundings because their trauma goes unrecognised most of the time. But the damage can be as much. This is common in people who see their loved ones suffer closely - caregivers or those who are put in the position of being the problem solvers but can't really solve the problem. Those with survival guilt. Or the guilt of not being able to help enough. Fear, anger, grief; it can be a mix of emotions that causes this to get rooted deeper in the person.

The third, largely undiscussed, is what I call *Shadow Trauma.* It is when a trauma victim is shamed, blamed and denied the voice to share that trauma. Where perpetrators spread narratives that keep the victim in a defensive mode, justifying their truth, constantly having to convince the world of their pain, while the shaming continues. Strangely, a victim is expected to look and behave in a certain way. Being sad, seeking sympathy, and looking impacted or damaged is the way people often assess victims. If you are a victim of any trauma, assault, abuse, etc, and have decided to heal your life and make it better, you are not given the right to talk about it anymore!

We live in a society where lines like a victim "asked for it" is the worst kind of shadow trauma impact.

Trauma remains the single largest cause of why people keep themselves away from goodness. From being wealthy, from being happy in a relationship, to having the health they want and deserve.

Take this Quick Test to locate where yours might be:

1. Have you experienced the death of a loved one in your inner circle before you attained the age of 10?
2. Were you abused in any way as a child? [emotional abuse is observed to be far more damaging than physical and so subtle we often don't realise it till we dig deeper.]
3. Have you been shamed for any attribute? Body shamed, shamed for your voice, colour, height, facial features, body language, gender identity, etc.

4. Have you had a divorce, break-up or the loss of a loved one, which impacted you deeply?

5. Did you ever want anything really bad and attempted to get it for a long time but eventually gave up or are still trying but don't have it yet? [singles wanting to be in a relationship, individuals wanting to have a child, people wanting to do business but not having been able to, trying to make a relationship work, wanting to do something for a parent and losing the parent before they could, wanting to move to a place of choice and not having done that, etc.]

6. Do you have any health issue which holds you back from living a full life?

7. Do you have someone very close who had or has any of these, where you want to help and resolve it for them but are unable to? [Secondary]

8. Are you a victim and are being shamed or blamed for what has happened to you? Either by denying the event or by making you sound responsible for it. [Shadow Trauma]

What's the most common thought that would arise? Ok, maybe, you do have some small unprocessed emotions that you had forgotten about. Anyway, what does it have to do with money? How does this keep you from being wealthy?

Let me explain this with an analogy. Imagine a glass jar that is empty. And you have nice colourful pebbles and collector-grade crystals with you. You decide to put them into the jar and make it decorative. When you open up your collection you find a lot of different kinds of stones and trinkets in there that you decide to fill in. You empty the entire collection into the jar and then, realise that some of the pebbles that you had, had sand on them. The sand is now mixed in the jar with everything else. It has filled up the crevices and gaps available all through inside the jar. Although the jar looks perfectly fine and maybe a guest won't even notice it, you can see the specks in there and you know it has made its way inside the jar on all your treasures.

Memories from unprocessed emotions are like that sand. At first, they do not even appear, and even when they do, their impact is so little that we know nobody else will notice them and so, we let them be, move on with our life, learn to shove it under the carpet because the new world has sold us this "happy pill of positivity" where we are almost compelled to be and show positivity even when we are breaking inside. And so, we carry on with things tucked in. But the sand remains, filling those crevices and making its way to leave a mark on everything it touches and settles on. And some day, most of us want to go back and clean that jar again, get the sand out, and rinse the jar and all the treasures maybe, so that we can live whole again!

And why is this cleansing necessary to actually live a fulfilled life?

Remember, money problems are never really about money?

In these chapters, we delve deeper into how some of our stories, beliefs and experiences can come in the way of finding our own fulfilment and how it shows up in the way we receive money and prosperity in our lives.

Trauma is associated with emotions. Good and bad memories create emotions the same way. These memories get stored in our mind and also our body. This is the reason why an emotion affects our bodies even more obviously than our minds. Given every trauma we have ever experienced is stored somewhere in the body. It is already filling the crevices and taking shape. It comes up and makes us do or keeps us from doing things time and again, sometimes pretending to be our inner voice. Before we know it, we are in the spiral of patterns that we are unable to break.

A friend who saw his father bring their entire family down to the last penny due to some horrible business risks he took still carries the fear of losing all he has, the shame of having to ask people for help and the anger towards his father for letting their family go through that. He hasn't been able to process it all. The result being, in his 40s now, he still is jittery to make decisions, he is feverish about making money but finds himself getting cold feet whenever he explores an opportunity and he backs off at the last minute. The trauma resides so deep that in his mind he has equated business and new attempts to failure and shame. And although he has forgiven his father at a superficial level for the mistakes [because of course they were well intended] at a deeper level, he holds resentment towards his father too.

Unknowingly, he is walking in the same footsteps. He is repeating the mistakes his father made with repeated wrong decisions.

Can he change his history?

No, he can't. But he can heal the memory and release his emotions. And let the trauma be processed so it can leave him – in mind and in the body. Absolutely.

By being aware of his pattern, by looking at his scars, he can heal and let the past go. Only then can he really build from a space of new. Most people don't acknowledge the problem. And then, obviously, there can then be no solution.

Physical Responses

Most of our memories, good and bad, get stored in our bodies. The reason why sometimes we feel a range of emotions suddenly emerge when put in a familiar place or around people we once knew even if we are not in touch anymore. The proof of this is that sometimes, these are outside the purview of what we "know" or "remember." A place we had been to as an infant or toddler maybe, it is not in our processed memory, and yet, it may trigger a range of emotions that we can't understand when we visit that place as adults. An emotional déjà vu!

Have you experienced this?

Remember suddenly bumping into a childhood neighbour whom you have warm memories of on a winter morning and feeling that warmth and immediate feeling of comfort you can't explain? It's like a freshly brewed favourite beverage handed to you. That's how fragile our emotions are. And these get stored somewhere in our body too.

These serve both as the result and sometimes as triggers for further responses that may arise, if the memory is negative, such as in the case of a trauma.

The most commonly accepted physical symptoms that may result due to unresolved traumatic events may be:

Headaches, heartburn, increase in heart rate, digestive issues, sweating and fatigue.

I am not a medical expert and it is outside my purview to talk about how the medical outcomes may be resolved.

I restrict to my topic of how the subtle experiences that scar us and are not even recognised as "trauma" in our society can impact our lives. And more importantly, we might find our own mechanisms to recognise, acknowledge and release them so that we can move into our zone of performance.

This chapter outlines a few predominant emotional states with the physical and mental responses that people might have, only to assist us in identifying and recognising our very own version of the emotions we are still to process.

The Most common Unprocessed Emotions & How They May Manifest

Fear

Fear resides in our minds and bodies both. Mental health practitioners believe that people who hold a lot of fear inside them tend to develop not only a mindset that keeps them from doing things but also a physical stiffness that usually results in illnesses in the body.

Other than the medical and the more technical side, fear – in the most mundane form – comes in the way of living a full life. A fearful child will not enjoy the childhood games fully. They will not swing fully or get down the highest slide in the park. They won't try the roller coaster when everyone their age is. They won't play with dogs or ride horses or jump into a pond. They are often the ones who may stand in a corner and watch as the others play, and fight an inner battle between their desire to join them and the fear of hurting themselves.

As we grow up, this fear can take a more serious place in our lives. For many, it can take centre stage. It can extend into how we make our decisions, the choice of career, the risk we are able to take, the partners we choose and how we lead our life.

Fear can often take the form of "everything that can ever go wrong, will go wrong for me!"

On the vibrational chart, fear is at the frequency of 100/1000. Where 1000 is the ideal vibrational frequency of enlightenment.

What are you scared of? We all are of something.

As a child, I was fearless, the daredevil as many called me. In those days, it also meant "tomboy," a term I dislike to this day because it seems to imply that only boys can have all the fun! I have tried some crazy scary things as a child without really telling anyone at home.

Stretching my own limits and testing how far I can go was a favourite hobby. Quite literally. Whether it was riding bicycles on a challenging terrain when the cycle itself was not equipped for it, or stapling my finger to check if the pin can really go into human skin [a bet I had with someone]. Or dangling from the window of our fourth-floor apartment with no safety grill or belt to see the world bent upside down [until my mom caught me doing that and that openable grill was sealed forever.] Scraped knees, bad injuries...handling pain with ease were something I was proud of. I loved animals and tried riding early. I did some adventure sports that I wasn't even fit for or trained to do.

Despite all this, I had fears. Deep down, unearthed and latent. A fear of abandonment, fear of losing loved ones. Fear that I wouldn't be able to protect myself from my surroundings. Fear of abuse, the noise and screaming. Fear of entering old age homes or orphanages. I had many.

Over the years, I have had to work on many of these by doing a lot of inner work and was assisted by therapy in the more recent years. If I tell you I don't have them anymore, it would be a lie. It is work I do constantly. A little here and there, every day.

Micro fears are the everyday ones. Being scared of pets and animals or heights. Not trying adventure sports, or not trying new things can hamper and impact the obvious quality of life. Micro fears can keep us locked up in a small world because anything outside our comfort zone feels difficult to survive in.

Macro fears, like the ones I had, can hamper our deeper sense of life and fulfilment. It might lead us to do irrational things, handle relationships imperfectly, hurt people we love and get hurt by people in return. These can also lead us to make decisions that can have a much larger impact on our lives, while on the surface, everything might look smooth.

On a physical level, Fear **weakens our immune system** and can cause cardiovascular damage, gastrointestinal problems such as ulcers and irritable bowel syndrome, and decreased fertility. It can lead to accelerated ageing too.

Guilt [30/1000]

Guilt is another volatile emotion that can create havoc if not handled early on. To some extent, we all might have small specks of guilt in us. But the more pronounced ones can be triggered by a loss of a loved one, a divorce between parents, a joint family break-up, feeling jealous of a sibling you are supposed to love, etc.

Losing a loved one is a difficult thing at any age. And medical practitioners agree that in most cases, the grief is accompanied by underlying guilt. How pronounced this might be can differ from case to case. If there is an obvious causal relation to this loss, the guilt can be more severe than if it is a natural death.

The families of those who die by suicide might have extremely high levels of guilt as compared to those that die a natural death. The same might apply in case of an unnatural death such as in accidents or calamities, especially for the person who may have been driving or might have been with the deceased at that time.

Of course, the guilt has no correlation to whether there was really any fault or connection to cause it. Most often, it is only a play of our own minds that makes us feel guilty. As most faiths and science both believe and re-affirm that when the time to leave comes, people leave.

In such scenarios, people often develop survivors' guilt too. People who lose a loved one in an event which they too were a part of can tend to carry the guilt that they survived while their loved one didn't.

Human emotion is layered, and as one digs deeper, we might find layers of small stored emotions that we don't even recognise on a day-to-day basis. But it continues to play out and impact how we live our lives and relate to the world nevertheless.

Another form of unprocessed guilt is common in kids from broken families. A divorce or an abusive relationship between parents can often make the child feel like they are responsible for it. This layers a deep sense of guilt and even a question of their worthiness. In the longer run, these kids have a tendency to create and repeat similar patterns in their own relationships too.

They can push opportunities, money and even people away because deep down, they don't believe that they deserve it. Guilt can also lead to feelings of anxiety, depression and stress including difficulty sleeping, loss of interest, fatigue, difficulty concentrating and social withdrawal. Guilt can have a serious impact on a person's overall well-being.

Processing one's guilt and finding relief can be a transformational moment in life.

Humiliation/Shame [10/1000]

Shame comes at the bottom-most rung of the emotional frequency chart. Shockingly lower than grief, guilt or fear. This also means that it is one of the strongest negative emotions humans have.

That's probably why targeting someone's dignity or self-esteem has such an impact on the human mind that it can erode a person completely.

When it comes to money, shame can also appear in the form of embarrassment. Have you ever felt the embarrassment of being too rich or too poor? Realising you had too much when you went out with friends and saw one of them scrambling to shell out their share?

Or maybe, you grew up in a difficult situation, and every time you were invited to a party, you had to think about what amount you would need to spend there and thus, backed out?

In the society we live in, people are often shamed for various attributes. Body shaming, colour shaming, shaming for sexual orientation or race and many other reasons are common. In recent years, many voices have come up that are fighting these causes.

Shaming can leave a deep impact on the mental health of a person, sometimes taking decades to heal. Much of shaming can actually tread into the area of verbal abuse.

At a subtle level, in the long run, constant shaming can make individuals want to hide, and fear of being visible may set in. Anxiety in wanting to justify their actions repeatedly and the habit to seek validation of their own worth can be an impairment.

Shame produces an implosion of the body: head lowered, eyes closed or hidden, and the upper body curved in on itself as if trying to be as small as possible (the bodily acting out of the wish to disappear.)

People who live with shame often feel worthless, depressed and anxious. Shame can be a contributing factor to depression, anxiety and low self-esteem. People who are constantly ashamed live out a difficult emotional and mental battle each and every day.

Anger [150/1000]

Anger is an emotion that each of us is familiar with. To various degrees, we have all been at the giving and receiving end of it. Anger can be a very powerful emotion that, if channelised, can actually be motivational too. However, the frequency of anger is much lower than the ideal emotional frequency anyone would like to be at.

The role that anger can play in relationships, money and health is already documented and well known. Spurts of uncontrolled anger, even if followed by regret, can sometimes damage things beyond repair. Anger at oneself or at others can build a lot of stress in the physical system and put pressure on mental health too.

It tends to impact the way we behave, speak and relate to the world. Both in personal relationships and in the case of career-related communication, anger has been observed to be a huge impacting factor.

Angry people are resentful and often do not have the presence of mind in decision-making. When we are angry, it changes our state of being and makes us unstable. Like many other unprocessed emotions, anger can run deep. The memories and stories sections in this book can help you dig deep and unearth many emotions under the surface.

The long-term physical effects of uncontrolled anger include increased anxiety, high blood pressure and headache. Anger can be a positive and useful emotion if it is expressed appropriately. Long-term strategies for anger management include regular exercise, learning relaxation techniques and counselling.

The best way to step out of chronic anger zones in your life is to forgive yourself and those you are angry with. I am not implying condoning anyone's actions, but simply not letting their hold on you to continue. Forgiving them is just about enough to let that anger not control you anymore.

Reversing this, taking charge of the anger inside can help you channelise it productively into a fruitful fight for a goal you might want to achieve.

Grief [75/1000]

Grief is an inevitable part of life. Most human beings have experienced or will experience grief in some form, at least three times in their lifetime.

Like every other emotion, grief also can be for multiple reasons and is known as a deep sense of loss accompanied by sorrow/sadness which lasts for a while. The frequency of grief is low and it can feel draining or even closed to the rest of the world for a person experiencing grief.

There is often a sense of being unworthy of getting good things and a proportion of disappointment when it comes to grief. People tend to keep themselves away from the good things when they are battling with this emotion.

The fact that a loved one is not with us anymore might subconsciously keep us from upgrading and enjoying life fully. The fact that our loved one is not around to enjoy it anymore, can keep us from enjoying it too.

Remember, nothing is right or wrong. They are just feelings and blocks we collect, and becoming aware and letting go can bring freedom.

In the long run, grief can have a heavy impact on the mind and the body. People with unprocessed grief can sometimes indulge in self-pity, and with time, this can become a habit. With months and years of grief becoming a habit, the spiral gets extremely difficult to break, and there is a certain impact on wealth, relationships and health.

Grief can cause a variety of effects on the body, including increased inflammation, joint pain, headaches and digestive problems. It can also lower immunity, making one more susceptible to illness. Grief also can contribute to cardiovascular problems, difficulty sleeping and unhealthy coping mechanisms.

What Do Unprocessed Emotions Have to Do with Money?

Remember, money problems are never about money!

Deeper down, what we think of ourselves and the world around us, how we think about people, our communication and thoughts. What triggers us and what elevates us. How open we are to receiving. How free we are mentally to be ourselves. Basically, how baggage-free we are. These things determine what we make of our lives.

People who have unprocessed emotions often live in a world of their own with pre-conceived notions of how things should be. Their own experiences come in the way of how they make decisions and how they deal with the eco system around them. Their subconscious minds often throw up behaviours that stem out of these stored emotions and because they are unaware of these at the fore, they often behave and show up in a way very different from how they might want to.

The way we show up shapes our world and forges our relationships. It is an important skill to find success in any area of our lives. Finding ways to harmonize and synchronise our emotions from time to time is an important step to keeping ourselves empty and clean to handle the world better and create better results for our lives.

Knowing Your Vulnerable Emotion

Another dimension to understanding how our emotions work is to avoid them from working against us. We all have certain emotions that are triggered in us easily. It can be more than one, but one is surely there.

For me, that one is anger. I can be easily provoked and my anger can be easily triggered. I have had to do a lot of work with harmonizing my emotions and stepping back time and again whenever I realise someone or even a situation is triggering anger in me. It can put me in a state of being where I can go back many steps from where I am at energetically and realistically too.

Fear or guilt or any other emotion might not be my point of vulnerability. I am more stoic with these, even if I am provoked. I can walk away from them.

The vulnerable emotion is the one we have to be most vigilant about. With time, people are also able to spot what this is in us and those who want to can use it to exert power over us. So, becoming aware of our vulnerable ones and doing additional work on them can keep us prepared for unexpected situations.

Techniques to Recognize and Befriend Your Emotions

I share some common techniques which I have used and which have been of tremendous help to millions of people across the world, in the chapter called "Support

Toolkit." These help in synchronizing and harmonizing our emotions and releasing them time and again to lead a better life at both micro and macro levels.

In this chapter, I also introduce you to a concept that I use whenever I am identifying and releasing any money-related blocks. The OZR method, acronym for Origin-Zero-Rewire, is a system that works on the principle of finding the origin of the emotion or story.

Origin ~ Whenever you are working with a Memory or Emotion, dig deeper to go back to the point where you think it originated. There would be a point where you remember the memory from. That is the point of origin. Even for an emotion which is deep-rooted, you can identify the point where that would have first germinated inside you. Remember, the origin is always your version of it and not what was necessarily a fact. So, we are not looking for researched facts or timelines, we are only looking for your perception of them.

Zero ~ Once you find the origin, your effort is to use whatever methods you can to release it. Several techniques like journaling, EFT, Sudarshan Kriya and more are given in the support tool kit. They can be very helpful in bringing that memory or story down to zero [or the closest to it]. Zero is the state where our focus is on emptying out that negative perception that resides inside us such that we could free up space for what we want to fill it with.

Rewire ~ This is the point where the practices in the Support Tool Kit continue to keep you free from negative impressions on a consistent basis and the work on the transformational tool kit help create new muscle memory and build healthier and more fulfilling outcomes.

OZR is something we will continue to refer to repeatedly in the upcoming chapters too.

Worksheet Emotions [Origin – Zero – Rewire]

1. What is your Vulnerable Emotion? [The one that can be triggered/provoked easily, that can be used to overpower you - could be more than one].
2. List three emotions that you experience intensely and often [spot repeated patterns and those that recur. A response to an event which happens and goes away naturally is not what you are looking for].
3. Look these up on the Emotional Frequency Chart to measure the work you might need to do in order to go up towards the positive zone.
4. Against each, find the Point of Origin.
5. Get to Work ~ OZR

From the Support Tool Kit
EFT {Emotional Freedom Technique}

- Although this technique might look weird or uncomfortable at first, it's because we often find it difficult to tap into the abstract. EFT or Tapping as it is called is an ancient technique coming out of Acupressure and the Power of Affirmations rolled into One.

- Many leading sportspersons, international players, actors and musicians frequently use this technique, sometimes just before their match or concert which you will be able to observe. In the last few years, EFT has become mainstream with a lot of people across the globe practising it.

- The process is simple, where we tap using fingers of one hand [or both] on various meridian points while saying an affirmation either aloud, or in our minds.

- As we tap on each point while repeating the affirmation, it is said to relieve us from the intensity of the emotion that we are feeling through acceptance and release. What is interesting is that the affirmations in this process cover and specifically mention the negative emotions that you are feeling. Acknowledging them before proceeding to release them through rounds of tapping.

On Each Point, we can roughly Tap about 6-8 times. The Points to be tapped one after the other are:

- Karate Chop Point (in line with the little finger on the side of the palm).
- The eyebrow, where your eyebrow begins from the centre, on the bone there. Both can be done simultaneously.
- Temples. Can be done on both sides simultaneously or on any one side.
- Below the eye, on the cheekbone. Again, either both sides or one.
- The bridge between your nose and lip, in the centre. With either hand.
- Between the lip and chin.
- Collar Bone. Both or one side.
- Below your Arm Pit, on the side of your Torso. Both or one side.
- On the top of the head with one hand, centre.

All the points done in the above sequence complete a round.

When you are feeling too emotional or any strong emotion feels intense, you can do about 10 to 12 rounds of tapping to feel a difference. You might like to mark where you rate the emotional disturbance on a scale of 1 to 10, before and after tapping.

Doing tapping as a routine can also be part of your daily emotional health regime.

Affirmations/Scripts

Although what you say would largely be connected with how you are feeling on that day, I am sharing some indicative scripts for an idea. You can also look up online with searches for what exactly you want to tap for or what emotion you want to process or the result you want to achieve that day. Several scripts and demonstrations are available.

"Although I am feeling anxious and restless right now, I completely love and accept myself."

"Although I am not regular with my workout and not following a diet, although I know that I might never do as much as I should for my fitness, I completely love and accept myself."

"Although I don't like that I am not disciplined and waste time, I completely love and accept myself."

The key to this process is to close each point with a statement of self-acceptance and love and then, move to the next. Mention the negative feeling, emotion or even what seems like a fact to you then and follow up with "I completely love and accept myself."

The idea is, over time, although you acknowledge your flaws and whatever else is negative, you accept and love yourself unconditionally. Unconditional love can be the key to complete inner transformation.

Chapter Summary

- *Know your Vulnerable Emotion so that you can be aware when it is taking control of you.*
- *Practice EFT whenever you feel overwhelmed with any emotional turmoil, and as a daily routine to maintain balance.*
- *Find the Original Point of the Emotions that you find predominant. What was the event that triggered it that keeps it inside, unprocessed? What does it trigger?*
- *Breath Work is one of the best ways to deal with Unprocessed Emotions and even Trauma. The Support Toolkit has some recommendations.*
- *If you desire to work deeper on this and stay updated, you might like to connect with us.*

Chapter 2.3
Reframing Money Stories

"We all have issues because we all have a story. And no matter how much work you have done on yourself, we all snap back sometimes. So, be easy on yourself. Growth is a dance, not a light switch."

Stories can be fascinating tools to transform and we all have many. Something an uncle said when you were 4, or another thing your grandmom kept saying to instil morals in you but you took away something completely unintended from it.

Even a story from a movie, a book or something narrated by someone else.

Most of the time, the story is not yours. And many times, the story is nothing but your perspective of a completely different situation.

One of my many stories comes from something I read about a multi-millionaire industrialist in India many years ago. One of the two known brothers, sons of an equally well known and successful father. I read in one of his interviews where he narrated a transformational moment for him.

He spoke of a time he led a client meeting where he was presenting and pitching for closure and was sure it went off well. When the meeting concluded and he walked out of the room, he overheard the client say "He's someone who can't take care of his waistline. How will he take care of the topline in business?" Boom. Powerful line, a punchline really. But what did that mean for the industrialist? He says he began his fitness journey and even went on to become a marathoner in the following years. He got his waistline under control. That was HIS story.

It became mine. But because it was in my subtle consciousness, I did not realize it enough to get up and create a transformation or work on the waistline. Instead, I built my version of that story. Until my waistline is not within my control, how would I be able to manage toplines.

Do you ever feel that how you look, the colour, weight, height, ethnicity, gender, sexual orientation, the language you speak, the country or region you come from or anything which is a visible fact about you, comes in the way? Do you believe deeper that until these things remain you are not going to be able to succeed or be wealthy? What is it keeping you from?

I realized with a lot of inner work and with experience over the years that digestive metabolism might not come easy to me but I am great with Financial Metabolism. Give me a million and I can make it 10. I can coach others to make it 10 too! My waistline has nothing to do with it! While I might still want to work on the waistline part, it does not reflect my capability or capacity to succeed or be wealthy, or even assist others to be both.

Worksheet – Let's Find the Stories

Write out 5 stories from your early years which play up. It is the story you might need to unearth; it might not be easy in your memory. You can find it by starting to write a list of memories from your past. If you have already done the memory work, you can go back and read that part. You can mark against each memory if you had made a story from it.

Another way to find your stories might be in your own words - the common phrases and lines you heard as a child that pop up in your conversations even today. The versions you carry from simple things you picked up from your surroundings.

Maybe "you can't have the cake and eat it too!" or "don't tell others when you make a wish, or it won't come true!"

Remember, like in every other place, your sensory superpower is going to be your partner in unravelling this too.

Around money, love, family, relationships, journal based on these prompts. Don't make any point long, just a gist in less than two lines is enough. You can elaborate on it later. For now, just list out memories around criticism or negative comments from others or yourself about yourself to see what story may have formed around it.

Pick five most prominent ones. The ones that repeat – the ones that show a pattern of returning. There's no rule to pick these. Just pick up what resonates as the strongest. Take these five and write the memory in detail with the story around it. For example, in the above instance. My memory might be the article I read. The story I created is "if I want success and wealth, I need to lose weight" or even more so "until I don't get my waistline in shape, I can't be wealthy or successful."

And the most prominent way in which it showed up for me was in my avoidance of being too visible.

What are the conditions you have set for yourself? What has to happen before you can find success and wealth? How is this playing out in your life today? Where do you hold yourself back or block your own growth? What is the repeated pattern you see in how wealth and success treat you?

What was Your Family Story About Money?

Most families have a story that has been passed on from one generation to the next.

One of my neighbours had a story that people in the pursuit of money and success often abandon their closest relationships, and the suffering then continues for the years to come. Their grandfather had abandoned his family, leaving on a certain day suddenly, never to return. The uncertainty of losing someone with no emotional closure can be a devastating experience.

Breakups, divorce and even death offer closure. With time, survivors learn to deal with a new normal viz-a-viz what was because they know what happened. But when someone we love just disappears – no questions asked, no answers given and there's uncertainty around it – it can be far more traumatic.

This family never quite recovered from it. The sons and daughters and their own families also carried the story forward, tweaking it in their own way. The lady of the house had never even met this man, her father-in-law. Yet, this crept into her conversations regularly.

In my family, we had a story that a lot of wealth can lead to conflicts in the family and spoil relationships. This was despite the fact that the families are close-knit and logically money friction hasn't usually come in the way. When I went back into the story further, I realised that the roots of this were three generations past.

My maternal grandfather chose to join the INA [for the unversed, the Indian National Army formed by Subhash Chandra Bose in the Indian Subcontinent in the 1930s] and chose to fight the World War II on behalf of INA, which was representing the Japanese with a bid to negotiate Independence for India in return.

He was a Law Graduate and was a determined and brave man. He went to war in 1942, and a few months from then, he, unfortunately, went missing. He disappeared leaving his wife, an equally determined woman, and three young kids – all below the age of 10 - behind. The next five years were an unexpected twist of fate for his family back home.

As months passed, his seniors and others were almost sure that he should be declared dead. However, as per the law, the matter was left open for the subsequent years. Five long years later, he emerged. His kids were older, his wife carried a visible sense of exhaustion trying to prove to the world that he was going to come back. Behind that inner smile was the burden of handling those staring eyes and those glares questioning her presence on happy occasions. A "widow" according to them and not dressed up like one.

We can only but imagine the humiliation and insults hurled. [In the 1940s and for many decades after, becoming a widow or losing one's husband has been a heavy burden for an Indian woman to carry. Differing mildly from region to region and also from the level of exposure, education and cultural evolution, by and large, a widow who doesn't carry herself like one, unfortunately, can still attract judgements and criticism.]

What might be the story that her three young kids created with this experience?

What might have been a story she wrote from it?

My mom was born a year after my grandfather returned. For her, this entire ordeal is a narration she heard, not having experienced it herself. What might have been her story?

Everyone who might have created or read the situation differently might have built different versions – their own versions of the same event.

In those long five years, all they had was each other. My grandfather's choice of going to war also meant that the authorities took care of the families left behind.

Food supplies, education and everything were being provided for. In one sense, they had access to a better life, but the uncertainty kept them unhappy and in a feeling of insecurity and lack. Was this the interpretation they made? When the money arrives, does it take away relationships and people from you? How would it have shown up in their lives?

Although all of the family streams did considerably well and remained close-knit, I wonder how their lives might have been different, if one decision made by my grandfather had been made differently.

Of course, my study in hindsight of that situation is only a theory, academic. I can't even start to imagine how difficult that time might have been for the family.

Family Trauma and even National Trauma can be real and move from generation to generation. These stories can often become an "Invisible Heirloom." Something that might bring an extremely positive emotion superficially – in this case, pride for the valour and the grace with which he carried himself – but deep down, it might leave scars that remain unacknowledged and unprocessed. Unknowingly, we may pass it on generation after generation until someone stands up and faces it head-on, questions it and becomes aware of the damage. Awareness is the essence and the beginning of healing.

Why are Stories Important?

Our stories play a large role in how we look at the world and how we perceive that the world is looking at us. It influences our beliefs, our memory structure, the rules we set for ourselves and even our emotions. If you observe similar traits in members of a family who live in the same place and have the same experiences, it's often the same not only because of heredity but also because they carry the same story. If it was heredity or the genes, it would have reflected the same way in members even if they were dispersed across different geographies. Again, since genetics is not my subject, I am speaking from the perspective of stories alone!

This also explains why peer groups have such a deep influence on us. We carry the same stories about many things and shared belief systems too. Our stories also become the filters with which we see the world and often, these filters determine our experiences and the repeated patterns that we see.

Money being Evil or the Rich being Evil is a story prevalent in most parts of the world. If that's a story you grew up with, you most certainly carry a resistance inside you and keep too much money away. Even if, on the surface, you actually work to get more of it and wonder why it isn't happening just as yet.

The Most Common Money Stories That Can Block Your Growth

1. Money Spoils relationships and creates Conflict.
2. Money is evil and the rich are evil.
3. I would rather be a good person than a rich person.
4. I want to do good in the world; money doesn't matter to me.

5. There is so much poverty in the world; nobody has a right to be wealthy.
6. If I make too much money it will make me a bad person and it will corrupt me.
7. I am spiritual; money shouldn't matter to me.

You can add to this list and see how your money story reveals itself to you.

Social Scenario and The Movies

In a global context, you would have watched several movies and found how they characterize the wealthy. Most often, they are cold-hearted, even evil and exploit those they perceive to be below them.

In the 1970s, a lot happened in the geo-political scene in the Indian subcontinent. During the Industrial Revolution, with a lot of political strife, many sectors were taken over by the government and ceased to be open to private business houses causing an environment of dissent and conflict.

It was a time when the political and business affiliations were becoming obvious and the power play in the system was on the rise. This, in hindsight, was also a time when in this part of the world the rich got richer and the poor got poorer.

The movies reflected an extremely one-sided view of what the rich looked like and how they behaved. Some of the blockbusters of the 1970s in Bollywood clearly take the anti-rich and pro-labour class perspectives of narration.

The dissatisfaction in the minds of the common man was a breeding ground for upcoming scriptwriters and producers to make hay while the sun shines. Movies which narrated and widened the divide became popular. Eventually, that became the new blockbuster formula.

Almost every movie that you can look up in the 1970s – even of the megastar Amitabh Bachchan – displays the hero as the common man who has to "fight" the system. The system here depicts the evil industrialists and the politicians on their side.

One popular scene in the blockbuster of 1975 Deewar has become iconic and is still cited as one of the best-written and executed screenplays of all times. True that.

This scene is a dialogue between two brothers, both born to and raised by a single mother who can barely make ends meet. One who becomes the good cop [needless to say righteous and poor] and the other becomes the suave wealthy businessman [read "smuggler" – wealthy and with no ethics left.] The characterization of both the brothers by the two wonderful actors of Indian cinema who brought these alive onscreen in Amitabh Bachchan as Vijay and Shashi Kapoor as Ravi made the movie and especially this scene a hit. The scene is cleverly shot with the backdrop of the bridge, where both the heroes as kids were forced to live. This brings about a poignant angle to this scene.

The shortest string of dialogues go:

Vijay: "*mere pass bangla hai, gaadi hai, bank balance hai, tumhare paas kya hai... kya hai tumhare paas*" [I have a bungalow, a car and a bank balance. What do you have... what do you have?]

Ravi: "*mere paas maa hai*" [I have {our} Mother!]

This movie was released before I was born, but I can be sure that the cinema-goers would have whistled and clapped on this scene. To date, "*mere paas ma hai*" is considered one of the most iconic dialogues of Hindi cinema. Great for cinematic effect and for the impact it had on the common man watching this scene in a theatre. After all, Ravi's dialogue of righteousness and perceived superiority resonated much more with them than the now unethical and rich smuggler, Vijay.

It is debatable if those who whistled and clapped might have opted for honesty if they had a chance to take Vijay's route for survival! Notwithstanding the fact that Vijay had to face the odds, support his mother and brother, and face humiliation in the process at an early age. He was witness to how the world treated his mother, while Ravi was a toddler and not in the picture most of the time. If we look at the entire context of the story and that Vijay had little choice, the fact that his choices were driven by the instinct to survive – to get his family to survive – is missed. The fact that Ravi had things easier because Vijay made them so for him is overlooked. The scene and the movie, written for a single-screen audience and to milk the social rebellion of those times, look at the story from a single prism of right and wrong. Whereas, most people, situations and circumstances are grey.

I am sorry as this might actually pierce the silver-screen magic if you are a movie buff and many of the movies you thought were perfect might start opening up new aspects for you. And my intention is not to run something down; it is to recognize and help you recognize that the take home from many of the things and content fed to us might not be serving us. They, in fact, might be hampering us.

Learning to look at every story differently is your mind's workout to create new narratives of your own stories.

As you reframe your stories, remember ~ ***it is time now to script your Dream Life!***

Worksheet Stories [Origin – Zero – Rewire]

1. Write down the stories that have emerged from this chapter. Dig out more. Take your time. Come back to this exercise whenever you uncover more.

2. Against each, write down the impact it has had on you. What is it keeping you from? How is it holding you back? What do you do [or not do] that keeps you small?

3. On a fresh page, write your wiser, more adept version of the story. How do you see this story differently? What is your new version of it? This is rewiring and is the most important part of the process. Spend time on this. Use your sensory super power to internalize the new stories.

From the Support Toolkit

1. Reframe Exercise

- Pick a movie you really like. Any language, any kind which has a hero and villain set up. Suggestions could be Sholay, Mr India {this is because they are cult films in Hindi cinema and almost each of you would have seen them. Also, because the villains in these are larger than life.} If you are an English Movie Buff, you could pick Spiderman.
- The story we all know – the narrative in the movie as it pans out. Write that out in the shortest form you can in less than 10 lines. Bring out the glory of the hero and the wickedness of the villain. This is the story you know, the story you were fed and told – the story everyone knows about this movie.
- Write a different story now in more than 25 lines. This time, the narrative is of Gabbar Singh or Mogambo [your villain]. Take his narrative and make him the hero now. Maybe, he had a story that we never got to know. Maybe, he was abused by the system. Write details from his point of view.
- You can repeat this for different films, books or any plots you like. Go into detail about every point that you can use to glorify the villain.

2. Scripting

- Scripting is a different format of journaling. Pick a date. Maybe 3 months or 6 months from now. Or whatever time in the future.

- Write how your life is on this date in detail. Get into as many details as you can professionally and personally. How much money you have, what car you drive, what your business balance sheet looks like, what your marital status is, what your home looks like; whatever else that matters to you. This is a more compelling way of visualization with more details wired into your brain to start a new story!
- Remember to put your all into this.

Chapter Summary

- *Stories are the most powerful tools to transform your money situation.*
- *Reframe every story, argue from the point of view of the villain and see how you can find a new perspective.*

This is one tool that will throw up many perspectives every time you use it.

Chapter 2.4
Rewording Money Conversations

"The Illusion that Everything will just turn out Magically without having to Communicate: Thoughts, Feelings and Needs in a Relationship, is an Immaturity that will make True Connection Impossible."

- Kylo

Money and the Pivotal Control

I sat at the café waiting for my friend to appear. It had been more than two hours since our scheduled time, and the only reason I was waiting was that I had a book to finish and the coffee was great. Bengaluru is a beautiful garden city in Southern India that was once known for its lazy evenings, streets full of green, blossoming riot of colours and slow-paced life. This is why it attracted the affluent to settle there post-retirement.

Back to the present, it is now India's own Silicon Valley. It is the first city to have housed and been the catalyst to several IT start-ups in the 1980s [before the word start-up officially came about] and Bangalore (as it was called then) has made it into history for the way it nurtured and adapted to the Information

Technology influx in the country at that time. Today, it is a cosmopolitan city and is predominantly occupied by the youth. The retired affluent people, needless to say, have moved to the towns and hill stations skirting this beautiful city that retains its old charm despite all the development it holds in its lap!

I have spent most of my childhood summers here. So, the affection and some level of attachment are natural. Later on, in the last two decades, Bangalore also brought a special connection into my life, but more about that later.

So back to the café where I sit and wait for my friend. She is the quintessential Indian woman who many might think has a dream life. She completed her education, got married to a man of her parents' choice and settled in with three kids born in quick succession. When business and diversification demanded the family move to Bengaluru, she quickly adapted to that change despite having no connection, family, friends or the will to actually make the move. For many years that followed, I continued to know more about the city than she did. Being a homemaker and her kids growing up fast meant a lot of free time on hand with not much to do. She came from a rich business family and married into another! Most of our friends who she wasn't in touch with any more thought of her as having the ideal life. No struggles, nothing to fight for; basically, sorted.

As another 15 minutes passed, my friend walked into the café. In a span of seconds, it was as if life had gone back 20 years to our college days. The quiet, sombre girl who shied away from attention looked like a different person, but as time passed and we chatted, she came out to be just the same.

What unfolded in the next few minutes came as a shocker to me. This friend who comes from an extremely affluent family, raised with discipline but with a lot of attention and independence, didn't even know how her bank accounts were being operated! She had no access to her own accounts, hardly any disposable cash in hand ever and everything was "provided for" by her husband. She was covered in brands from head to toe. That solitaire on her finger…to me, came across as a little, shy, silent girl lost in a big world where she didn't know how to fight for herself rather than a symbol of love.

Why is this story even here in this book? Because this is the story of many women across the world; more so in India, where the system still is inclined towards traditional joint families. Large families doing business together is common. This also extends to women often times living with a large family and having fewer negotiation rights.

Money has an almost intrinsic connection to power and control. Sometimes, in an abusive manner and other times, in a constructive one. Many families believe it is their duty to provide for their daughters-in-law, and having done that, it might not even cross their minds that it isn't enough.

In many traditional relationships, money plays a role of the point of control, even authority. One of the reasons why the financial divide between a couple in the marriage can be an obvious deterrent unless both partners handle it in a mature and centred way from the start.

Between couples, the dynamics should be handled with more communication and discussions. Even in joint family environments, two people can pair up to understand and work their dynamics to assist each other and grow.

A typical couple issue is when both partners come from different money perspectives. Note here that we are not talking about money positions but the perspectives – how we perceive things to be.

When two people get together, they are able to see and spot the differences in their cultural and financial positions. The way money is discussed, managed or even spent in their respective families would play a role in their individual relationship with money. If both partners come from extremely different views and perspectives on money, the way they attempt to deal with it in their relationship might also be impacted.

Like in the case of my friend, both she and her husband come from families that have wealth, but their way of managing it and spending it is different. The power positions are different. My friend's family encourages the young to learn, grow and become decision makers. Her siblings are all pursuing their careers; one of the brothers is in the family business while others have gone into different streams in which they found their passion. In their family, money is a tool to improvise and grow and is a catalyst for a better life, which offers independence in both the choices they make and the lives they live.

Today, 4 of her siblings are married to partners of their choice and have dynamics they have built out of choice. Amongst all their spouses, only my friend's husband matches the stature of this family. This means there is no obvious financial divide but there is a huge difference in how their families handle money. This percolates into their personal relationship with money. And like in every other emotion we have, the money emotion also seeps into the closest relationships we have.

Marriage means, on average, 30,000 meals, on an average 2,500+ weeks, and unending conversations. It requires an understanding to take joint decisions in day-to-day ones as well as for those that would have a long-term impact. And this difference in money-related decision-making can also be deal breakers sometimes.

The Money Quotient Conversation

Emotions impact money and your money decisions much deeper than you know. Guilt, fear and anger can make you do things you might regret in hindsight. When two people start a life together, or whenever you realise (if you have already started your dream life together), plan a vacation where the two of you will go build a life plan around money.

The two most common reasons for parting ways or divorce in the world are around Money or Sex.

Read that again!

So, get the act together before you get there. For the latter, you can find ways outside of this book, since I would prefer to stick to my area of expertise.

Discuss this with your partner and plan a time out to have this chat. This is a conversation which can take hours, days or weeks depending on where you are at! This conversation must be made mandatory for all couples planning to live together, married or not! [Disclaimer: in a rare case, this might bring up a completely different level of gaps or disparities that you think you cannot bridge. That is not my suggestion, but it's always great knowing what you are getting into!]

- Suggest you both workout an individual plan for the next 1, 5 and 10 years [most people can't think beyond these time frames, if you or your partner can, then great! Go for it!] Do not discuss or create this together. This is Individual.

- Your typical agenda might include: Bank Accounts, properties you buy together, the home you intend to live in, your career plans, if and when you plan to have kids, your thoughts on helping family and friends and asking for help, Your Saving-Spending habits (good to have a point of reference of past 5 years), what your ideas about economy and luxury are, how invested you are emotionally in your families, what is your idea of handling an emergency and more that might be relevant to you.

- Once you have your own MQs handy and head for this discussion, remember the primary rule to keep any relationship flourishing [money or not] – do not get judgemental. If your partner has views that clash completely, it is still fine. An honest and open conversation can lead to common grounds.
- This holiday can be a ***Money Honeymoon*** where you both can actually work out a line of thought for how you, as a couple, will manage money and the decisions that come with it. This can be based on the money, intelligence and exposure that each of you has and on your skill sets.

My Mom and Dad had a clear boundary when it came to who handled what. Although he was the one who kept the cash flows going, she was the one who kept every other relationship and money decision going. They clearly knew that my dad would often get stuck in his habit of not saying no and land up then feeling resentful because he had lent money or invested in the wrong place. They came up with a plan where every decision for a request to borrow or invest to help someone out would come to the dinner table, and only when everyone had agreed, it would go through. Needless to say, if the family decided against it, the job to convey that 'No' to the person would be my mom's. But this arrangement worked great throughout their marriage where they earned, preserved and exponentially grew their money quotient in the almost five decades that they had together! Create boundaries, roles and responsibilities within the unit so that money decisions work seamlessly and creativity/productivity is not compromised.

Who Has More Money Vs Who Understands Money Better?

One of the errors in judgement most people make is that the ones who have more money necessarily understand it better. There is nothing farther away from the truth. Many people have an inherent understanding of money and how money works, even though they might not have access to a lot of wealth in any form just as yet. And many of us struggle with understanding the nuances despite being surrounded by wealth.

When two people from diverse financial backgrounds land up together, it might be an unspoken presumption that the one who has more money or has access to more wealth is essentially the smarter of the two when it comes to handling money. Sometimes, this presumption might also extend further when one of the two has an academic degree that warrants the understanding of finances better.

But both these can be faulty and, in fact, in cases like this setting, keeping the MQ in the beginning so you both understand who would be better at making the big decisions becomes imperative. Left undiscussed, the decision might invariably be made by the richer or the more educated partner, while the more sound and informed suggestion might be left out by both.

Evaluate this. Know who has what skill sets. Sometimes, individuals who see a lot of wealth early do not understand the dynamics behind it as much as those who have seen a struggle or been a part of it. This can lead to a twisted decision-making paradigm in the couple out of a misunderstood and often unspoken truth.

Some Points to Ponder

- Which of you can keep emotions out of Financial Decisions?
- Which of you is able to say no?
- Who, in the two, can maintain a larger proportion of whatever inflow they have in a month?
- Who between the two can spend on things that matter and bring you gratification while not going out of pocket or dipping into credit?

These can be markers to point out which of you is better at handling money.

You Might Not Play Power Games but the Money Creeps in

Power and Money are almost inseparable. Often, this equation leads to friction and conflicts in relationships. The power dynamics change where money enters. But sometimes, could it be that this is also a perceived control and not really the case at all?

What was the power dynamic around money when you were growing up?

Did you often see people with money also being powerful? And did you more often also see them misuse that power? If you are one of those who saw that, you would have emotion around money connected to power and control.

Sometimes, we can have extreme positions around it. Feverishness to be wealthy so that that power can be acquired because you believe there is no other way to get into a place of control. Or on the other hand, you feel helpless and powerless around people who you perceive to be wealthier than you. Which is more like you?

This power play plays up a lot in Indian weddings!

The Invisible Exchange

Love is a beautiful emotion. It brings with it the seeds of many risks and negative emotions too. I am a firm believer in forever love, which won't land up in legal battles, where we will willingly give away half of everything we have. Where fifty-fifty will never have to be negotiated. Where we will continue to stay well-wishers even if things didn't work out in the end. Where a piece of paper is not required to validate it.

But partnerships when made and when broken are not usually with the involvement of only two people. Families, friends and everyone around us have an opinion. And they give it! Under the spell of anger, hurt or grief, we often can be swayed away by what people around us feel and think and lose the connection with what promises we made. This can lead to decisions made under stress and under the current state of emotions.

Have a chat with a divorce lawyer and they can tell you crazy stories of how perfectly "in love" couples not only fall apart but become vengeful, bitter and behave completely illogically.

In any kind of partnership/relationship/marriage/live-in/civil union, there is an invisible exchange of faith and love and the will to make it work. Sometimes, there are practical reasons people consider to enter a relationship. The human mind is one of the most fascinating specimens to study.

When you are fed up and at the end of your wits, perhaps, you can take a break - some 'me time' - and list out 10 things why you got into this relationship in the first place. The 10 things you loved about your partner that are personality traits and haven't changed. If you can get 10 easily, try another 10. But if you can reach the first 10 easy, perhaps, you must rethink the idea of being "fed up."

Keep it simple. Talk. And then, talk some more. Have real conversations. Don't presume anything.

Parting Ways – keeping it Simple

The number of divorces that get contested over property divisions, alimony and maintenance are topping the charts in recent years. Couples, their families and kids from the marriage continue to bear the brunt for a long time. If you get deeper into this, if you were ever party to a divorce proceeding or saw one closely, you know that much of this comes from the fact that some topics were never discussed. The lack of communication around money. We live in a society that makes open conversations about money taboo. It glorifies those who put relationships first and almost demonises those who fight for what they believe to be their right. Even in cases where it truly should be.

Marriage is about love and sanctity; true, but there is a practical side and that can be – for a lack of a better word – described to be a contract. When two people build a life together [or attempt to], both bring something to the table. We don't expect to measure it or add clauses of the breach. So, the earning partner tends to believe they are doing more. At a different level, we all know and understand that there are many elements to keep a marriage and a family going. Some of which truly cannot be bought with money. When partners invest their time, energy and their best years in each other, money as a currency of exchange seems small in the poetic world.

But this very currency becomes the focal point of conflict the moment the relationship/partnership falls apart. Assets get valued and jewellery gets calculated, but the intangible elements partners have brought to the table are the sunk costs that can never be assessed or returned.

During the honeymoon period, it is natural and, perhaps, typical for people to not want to discuss separation or anything that might come out of it. But like everything else, this also is a difficult conversation that is a must-have. The amount of money spent on lawyers, on the collateral damage that comes out of the contested separation, can be saved and the turmoil and the connected trauma avoided just with clarity where it should ideally start. In the beginning.

Pre-Nuptial contracts, believed to be a gift from the west or "happens only in the rich" is a convenient way of looking away from things. Of course, whether to formalize a conversation and agreement between two partners in a prenup or not is a personal decision, but to avoid the conversation altogether is foolish, to say the least.

We live in times when tastes and likes change faster than the seasons, and it is only imperative for the security and protection of both partners to openly discuss what they would proceed to do and how they would divide joint assets and other financial areas if they ever parted ways. This is not an omen or not starting on a negative note. Like I reiterate in this book time and again, keep the emotion out of money!

What are the ideal discussions you might want to have before you enter into a formalized relationship [marriage, civil union, living-in or other depending on where you live and the context.]

1. Would you have Joint Assets or Bank accounts which shall be co-owned? In case of a Separation, who shall retain what and in what proportion?
2. Which of the two earns more and has a higher standard of living? Alimony and Maintenance is [rightfully] not only a right given to a woman

but also to a man. The one who earns more and thus provides a higher standard of living to the partner, can be asked to shell out towards maintenance/alimony. Where your relationship/ union is not formalised under the law, you might want to set out your own rules running parallel to how a prenup for marriage works.

3. If kids are involved, who shall get custody of the kids, or if joint custody, then how are the costs for the kids to be divided? Calculate living costs, education and other life milestones.

4. The Home you plan to live in… to whom does it belong originally and whose names shall it be on once you move there? This can have an impact on how the standard of living is determined.

5. Investments, club memberships, credit cards, home loans, other loans, life insurance, and nominations where one of you is the Holder/ Owner are some relevant topics to cover in this conversation.

6. What happens if one of you decides to walk out for no reason? What if one of you cheats on the other? How do you want to penalize infidelity?

Human behaviour and change are both unpredictable. Most contracts under the law fail to envisage every possible outcome because it is outside the purview of any logic to be able to account for or prepare for everything. But we can get as exhaustive as we possibly can stretch our minds in these conversations.

Nominations and Succession

Another difficult conversation, perhaps, even more tricky than a prenup is inheritance and the will. We all know we will pass away someday, and yet, we tend to think we have time on hand. In the last few decades, the age we are at has little to do with the time we have in hand. Every asset, immovable and movable, is handled as per the Succession Law that applies to you if you have not expressed your will in any format.

Recording nominations in Bank Accounts, Investments, and Immovable Properties ensure that you appoint a custodian to take charge and handle these assets as per your desired will. A *will* is a step further and is more conclusive in making your intent clear in writing.

In many countries, in India especially, the time and effort it takes to get one's claims honoured in case of the death of a loved one is a long and painful process. Putting a will in place and making nominations on all your accounts makes this process easier and simpler for people to handle. It also ensures that the law doesn't take its course and hand over any assets to someone who may be a "legal heir" as per the succession act but to whom you don't wish to give something.

In many cultures, discussing death and a will or related topics are as taboo as money and sex. But these are critical things that have to be discussed to safeguard the interests of those you love and yourself.

Remember – Keep the Emotion out of money decisions!

The Joint Family Dilemna

The joint family system, unique to a few select nations [India being one] brings with it its own set of challenges.

Families rarely discuss this. In large and supposed to be joint families, the main conversations around money and relationship issues usually remain buried due to the fear of being the black sheep if you bring this up. But bring it up and Boom! You will find everyone was secretly desiring to talk about exactly the same thing.

Uncertainty can be a deterrent to growth, both in careers and in marriages. Women getting married into such families often face the issue of not knowing what really belongs to them or their unit in the joint family setup. The fact that in traditional families, women are usually "permitted" to be home makers or have only sunflower careers, amplifies this fear.

They have access to everything but don't really own anything. Non-ownership takes away the right to make decisions. And decision-making and control are inherent human desires that nobody can fully let go off in their lifetimes.

Also, over and above this, there are legal rights and moral obligations available to these units within larger families, but talking about those or even getting better information about those might be considered rebellion. This is an effective societal way to keep the growing generations in check and within invisible walls as families and their businesses grow.

I had a friend whose joint family had a rule that the assets and the parts in the division of the family properties and businesses would only be given to those units that had a male heir within them. To put it simply, if any unit (read couple) did not have a son, they would not be entitled to any share or division should they separate from the family! They would only be "provided for" in their lifetime. Absurd and completely obsolete way of thinking, but this was as recently as two decades ago and no family member or unit questioned it or found a way out of it. But nobody agreed to it either. The ones without a son had resentment towards everyone else and the ones with a son had arrogance!

To me, it did not serve any purpose, because when conflicts grow within any group or organisation, it is the beginning of friction that will eventually take it and its members down. That is inevitable; only 'when' remains a question. The larger purpose of joint living and joint businesses when they started out was rather different. The context was to co-own, co-live and co-raise the next generation. Kids coming out of such families had a richer culture, better people skills and often exposure to different mindsets and points of view. Today, units within these larger joint businesses and families in conflict are filled with uncertainty and resentment, and in the end, the division is usually far from peaceful.

The Most Difficult Conversations in Families and How you could try to initiate

1. Division of profiles and drawings from joint businesses.

2. Fixed salary for the work done over and above the "share" or "rights" in the business.
3. Joint assets usage – Cars, holiday homes, memberships, holidays. The clearer you get the lesser chances of friction.
4. The most difficult and the largest elephant in the room – how are the assets going to be divided eventually if there is a split or after the lifetime of the head of the family?

Succession Plans, Will and Clear Demarcation on Personal Assets & Business

In the case of joint families, the impact and thus the need to do this is doubled. Here, every unit in the family might be looking out for clarity and some level of security in case the business splits up or if the future generations decide to divide it.

Within each unit, there can be independent dynamics at play, where the couple aspect comes in as discussed in the first part of this chapter. Given the complexity of these traditional systems of business and families, the conversations, however difficult, might have to be made.

The Elephant in the Room

If we had to make a list of things that we avoid talking about, the topic that is always the elephant in the room is certainly money; much more than sex, greed, deceit, or any other awkward conversation.

Board rooms have a curtain of formal protocols, families have their own context and stories which build the walls within which these conversations are permitted, couples would agree this is the single largest cause of fights, misunderstandings, comparisons and often difficult pieces of communication.

Learning and training ourselves to discuss money easily and smoothly and to make it a part of our daily conversations not only eases the stress of breaking the ice but also adds to more information exchange and eventually, superior decision making. Money can either break or build relationships. When people communicate more openly, discuss finances and plan together, the tendency to skirt around it vanishes in any encounter and the relationship can function in an easier space.

At work, at home and wherever Money has the potential to enter a conversation, make it a habit to be articulate in your communication around money. If you can build muscle memory around these conversations and begin to feel at ease around it, you would have resolved a large potential challenge that takes people a lifetime to do.

Worksheet
[Preparing for the Conversations]

- *Think of any two situations, [minimum] one personal and one professional, where you have discomfort or difficulty talking about money.*
- *Plan your script for these two situations and how you can handle them. Practice the script in front of the mirror as much as you can.*
- *You can make these two conversations once you finish this book.*
- *Share your experience with me @dhanashreebhatkal.*

Chapter Summary

- Build muscle memory to have money conversations.
- Assess your Money Quotient.
- Plan a money honeymoon.
- Script, practise and have that money conversation you have been avoiding after completing this book.
- Share your experience with us.

Chapter 2.5
Rewiring Money Beliefs

"What you are not changing, you are choosing."

Righteousness and Honour

Our beliefs are acquired from a time when we don't consciously know or realise them. Our early ones may be when we are a few days or weeks old and might only remain in our subconscious not fully grown or developed into our conscious mind in our entire lifetime.

Our parents and others in our circle of influence and later, our peers at school also impact these. Often, we carry our beliefs without ever assessing or even being aware of them. So, what was the narrative about honour in your family? What were the rules about how "we" do or don't do things? Most families have these, called traditions or simply "it's done that way" kind of hand-downs from our ancestors. Dig these out even when you think they don't matter.

Maybe, something like "It's bad manners to say yes to things when they are offered for the first time."

And if you are one of those who have heard this, you probably believe that you don't have a right to receive anything easily. Like when the first time something is offered to you, it usually means you don't really deserve it and the universe is only being nice. It is only on repeated insistence that you have any right to receive or enjoy it.

Of course, this does not mean our parents or elders were wrong in teaching us these etiquettes. But, perhaps, the lesson we picked from them was not what they wanted to teach us in the first place.

Traditions don't only come from families, they can come from various groups we belong to, where rules and traditions are put forth in a manner that we start believing we need to follow those in order to belong.

We had a tradition in my family. I remember when my cousins and I got back from school, my maternal grandmother would sit us down for a treat time once in a while. She would usually have just a few chocolates with her. She had seen tough times and resources had been meagre; it might have been a habit she developed then. The treat was meaningful for us since we knew she would usually save up to get us those. She would then break it into pieces and make sure each of us got an equal share. This tradition continued for almost everything that she had access to. Gifts on annual festivals and common events where kids are usually given new clothes or anything else. This was wonderful on one hand because she made sure nobody lost out and everyone was taken care of and got their share!

However, this also meant a deep-rooted memory for me [maybe, the others too!] This meant to me that whenever we had access to anything, it must be shared equally! It meant I would be a bad person if I enjoyed anything on my own or had more than the other kids in the family! It meant if I ever had access to something good that I deserved even, I still had to always share it with the others in order to follow and live up to my family tradition!

Boom. The day I realised and recognised this belief, I realised clearly all the zillion times I was giving things away and not receiving what was actually being dished out to me on a platter [sometimes, literally] simply because I didn't believe I deserved it. Especially, if I was the only one getting it or at least not until I had enough to be able to share it with everyone else!

Beliefs don't only come from family; they might be deeply embedded in our eco system. At school, in the movies and in the language we are exposed to.

Indians got independence from colonial rule in 1947 after a 150-year struggle for freedom. Our collective national emotion is patriotism. The system of beliefs around the British, around development, around our freedom fighters and the national flag are emotional conversations for most Indians. We are into the third generation and still only coming out of the shadows of deeply ingrained pain and tragedy that is spoken of. Even in the present context, this pain and struggle have been handed down to us. And when I think deeper, I wonder if the ingrained insolence and the way Indians like to break rules and rebel comes from that deep sense of years of struggle that we might still be carrying in our DNA. After all, we fought for more than 150 years for our independence. How many of us understand the responsibility that comes with freedom is another question altogether.

We have a rich culture and are traditionally a society which has been progressive and adaptive to make the best of whatever was thrown to us. But sometimes, it makes me think whether this is also the reason we are quick to adapt and move on even when things should be handled and faced head-on.

So, how do we tell between traditions that we must preserve and those that are hindering us?

Simple – look for what serves you. Very often, many of the beliefs we honour and go out of our way to adhere to, do not serve us anymore. Maybe, some never did. In fact, they may be hampering our growth or the way we relate to the world. They might be the reasons why we keep ourselves small.

Patterns and What They Might Be Trying to Teach You

Many a time, the patterns we repeat are the ones we are unable to repair. Until we don't release and rectify them, they will keep appearing in an attempt to teach us lessons.

What is coming back repeatedly in your life?

In your health, relationships, money, success in business or in your job, what are the events that have happened more than five times in your life in the last 10 years?

Can you look out for why they might be happening? What are they trying to teach you?

Some examples that you might want to use as a reference

1. Money getting stuck repeatedly with Family/ Friends/Clients [bad debt] – Is there a problem in receiving? Or are you trying to solve everyone's money problems?

2. Not enough paying clients [free jobs] – where do you doubt or carry a belief that charging money for what is a natural skill is wrong or equal to exploiting people?

3. Conflicts in relationships or a bout of ill health every time there is a financial gain – This is a problem of not believing that we can have it all.

   Look into your memories where you heard, "You can't have it all," "You have to compromise in life," and "Who do you think you are to have everything?"

   And so, every time you receive something in one area of your life, you sabotage it by losing out on another. Read *The Big Leap* by Gay Hendricks, which talks about this in great detail. It's a wonderful read if this is your problem area!

Choose Your Heroes Wisely

In the movies, in books we read and even in real life, we sometimes choose our idols based on what appeals to us. There is no reason why certain things might appeal to us more than others. Or is there?

We often see and hear stories in the context of our belief system which is set so early in our lives that we stop recognizing that the heroes we choose and aspire to be might not really be heroes we chose but they may, in fact, be an unknowingly led path. If we had family members in the army and sacrifice was a virtue that was repeatedly discussed in our homes, we probably look at sacrifice for the nation and bravery as the primary qualification in someone we begin to idolise.

If you saw early on in your family that education was important and the narrative always said to you "if you don't get a degree, you have nothing to fall back on," you probably believe that someone with academic qualifications is the one you look up to as your role model.

Our idea of "normal" comes from these belief systems and anything outside needs a conscious awareness for us to accept and internalise. Unless you identify and work on the norms, we may continue to filter what we see through the lens of our beliefs and choose to see selectively.

This might, in extreme cases, mean glorifying poverty, sacrifice, hardship and struggle. And in the long run, what message this really gives to your brain is that struggle is a pre-requisite to success. And every hero goes through extreme struggle in order to become a hero. This also means you are not a hero if you get anything easy!

How many of us have this?

I had it to a small extent. Although, I saw a completely transformed life between the age of 7 and 17. But I carried this feeling that the good don't have the money and those who do have money are not good.

"Giving is good! Compromise is Glorious! Putting others before you is supreme. You can either be rich or kind!" could be some other stories making you choose your heroes subconsciously.

For some, tragedy is glorified. Tolerance and courage are their superpowers. Being able to tolerate what normal people can't, gives them a kick. But does this serve them? Does pain really serve anyone?

The money personality we have might be both the result and the cause of our stories and the narratives that we make our own from these memories, emotions and beliefs that combine to form a concoction we can take a lifetime to understand. Recognising these personality traits, digging for those memories and then, rewiring our mind for the new script is essential for you to live your life to the fullest and find balance in your wealth, health and relationships.

Worksheet
[Origin ~ Zero ~ Rewire]

1. List out 10 beliefs you carry about money, success and having it all. [Ones that you now think are keeping you small].
2. Against each, mark out your first realisation of this belief and the impact of it you now see.
3. Bring it to Zero.
4. Rewire!

Chapter Summary

- *Righteousness & Honour*
- *Repeated Patterns*
- *Choose your heroes wisely*

Chapter 2.6
The Karma Angle

"The Moment you Start Acting like Life is a Blessing, it starts Feeling like One."

The universe is fascinating, and even more fascinating are all the narratives and stories that people make about it. Ancient cultures have always propelled and propagated the idea of "what goes around comes around" in some format or the other.

Hinduism – an ancient culture and more a way of life than a structured religion – has propounded this in a detailed format. Karma, today, is a word used worldwide and even has cafes and resto lounges named after it. Originally a Sanskrit word, Karma in its most simplified meaning is "Action."

In a more complex interpretation, it can mean many things.

But this book is about what serves us – what can prepare us for a better, happier life. So, we restrict the subject to only one aspect which is all pervasive and common place in terms of experiencing Karma.

Simply put, Karma is the closest cousin of the game of squash. You hit the ball; it comes back to you. The speed, force and angle are determined by how you hit it. This means, your action creates the reaction. This also means that how well you are prepared, how focused you are, your fitness, your clarity, the resources around you and your preparedness, have more to do with the outcome than luck!

In common parlance, many people equate Karma with luck/fate. It's quite the contrary. It is that element of the outcome which has a correlation to your action.

Pan out of the squash room and let's look at how this plays out in life.

Picture this. You wake up late and grumpy. Then, you remember you have an important meeting scheduled that you are surely going to miss. You get ready with the tension of the deadline running through your body. You get ready in a rush, you run out the door and realise you left your car keys inside. You rush back and storm back out in anger, at yourself, of course! You hit the road only to find that the traffic is higher than usual and it's not even the peak hour. You reach halfway to realize your fuel is low. That means another 10 minutes. You now are almost sure you will lose that contract.

Your phone rings, and you answer [on speaker, of course!]

It's your Executive Assistant calling to inform you that your meeting has been rescheduled by 2 hours since the client requested it. You hang up. You feel a clear loosening up of your system and your muscles around your neck ease up as you realize you don't have to rush anymore. Your temples relax, your jaw relaxes and you feel a sense of calm in the body.

The traffic eases out, you find no queue at the gas station and you get to work before time to settle in and prepare for that meeting.

One fact changes a stream of reactions in you. Your thoughts change, resulting in a new series of feelings, new responses and a new set of behaviours. The external stimulus [the call informing you of the meeting change] begins this process by infusing a new thought.

But what we often miss is that in the absence of a new fact that reveals itself, we can still bring about the same level of change by introducing a new thought or perspective. In a different scenario, people can train themselves and practice it until this new thought infusion becomes a habit.

The stimulus, instead of being external, can then be internal.

What is it that you give out every day? What is the energy/vibe you carry?

Have you noticed that on days when you start your mornings in a great mood - maybe you get up with a happy dream and wake up early to catch that extra bit of fresh air on a morning run - the entire day pans out smoothly? Obstacles and hiccups might, of course, occur but they settle faster and it isn't as upsetting for you as could be. Basically, you seem to be in charge of the situation rather than it being the other way around.

You are throwing a certain kind of energy out. And it comes back to you multi-fold.

This is also one of the reasons why the worriers and the overthinkers tend to almost always attract things that go wrong for them, which further strengthens their beliefs that if something can go wrong, it will!

We cannot take charge of anything other than ourselves: our thoughts, actions, behaviour and our energy. If we can keep ourselves clear, our intentions positive and always put our best out to the world, that is exactly what the universe returns to you.

The contrary is also true. Did you start a day on a bad note? Take charge and immediately re-align your energy before it spirals out into a bad day!

The Power of Giving

When I was growing up, I had an instinctive desire to share. Like I said elsewhere in this book, it was something my grandmom ingrained in all of us early on, but I do believe it was also a natural inclination that I had.

Nothing magnanimous or larger than life, but whatever I had access to. This is something I saw my mom doing a lot. She had big dreams of starting a foundation, but in those times, when we had shoestring budgets, she made sure to do whatever she could, for whoever around her needed it. She would say feeding one hungry person, educating one child, and helping one family in need also has value. It can have a percolating effect. She never waited to be richer or have more to do something for someone. This lesson has come a long way for me.

Without even realizing it, I got into the habit of doing small things whenever I could. When money was short, I could give resources that I had - time, energy, a shoulder to lean on, a hand to hold, a patient ear. ***It is amazing how the most valuable things we can give to people are abundant and free; we just don't realize it.***

Many years later, when I met a Holistic healer at a social gathering, she suddenly just shared this. She was telling this to someone else but I was there and I felt it was meant for me too. She said that ancient teachings believe that when we have less of something and really desire to attract more of it, we must share the same thing with those who have even lesser than us.

So, what she was suggesting is, that if my desire is to be wealthy, I might sponsor or donate, however small an amount, to someone who needs it more than me. If I am working towards better health, I could help someone to get healthier or fitter and so on and so forth.

It sounded interesting. In hindsight, I realized that what I had been doing without knowing this theory, without any focus really, had actually panned out in my life. Also, in my mom's life. Without even realizing it, wealth had flown into our lives and transformed our financial status by 180 degrees in the past few decades. I don't know for a fact if there was a causal relationship between this. But giving and doing good for as many as we can, in any case, is a very fulfilling feeling.

Giving essentially opens you up to receiving more. The need to hold on to something brings the feeling of lack. The scarcity mindset comes from the want to accumulate because somewhere down, you believe you might not get more. When you become an easy giver, the narrative inside you – your inner dialogue – changes. The freedom of giving brings with it the inherent freedom to receive freely.

So, either way, it is a win-win situation.

Do What Serves You

Some of us are inclined to be self-sufficient. To believe we are in charge and that we can have a causal effect on how our life pans out is a more fulfilling way for us. For some others, leaving things to the universe, or God, or a Divine Master, or even fate is what works better.

There is no right or wrong here. Take what serves you. If surrender serves you better, then do your part and leave it to faith. If you prefer taking charge, then do that and leave a little to fate.

There are many of us who think Karma is a mathematical account of lifetimes in which we take births in order to settle. There are varying opinions on whether this can be settled off in one lifetime or not. It's complicated. So, unless you want to study it for academic reasons, pick what serves you now. In the present. In this life.

If you live this life well, give all you can and receive all you can. If you keep great intentions, do good things, keep yourself on track, admit your mistakes and constantly work on becoming a better version of yourself, then the rest of your lifetimes will take care of themselves.

Our thoughts shape our feelings. Our feelings impact our actions and our inner dialogues. *The one place we live the longest and all our living years is in our head. It's our responsibility and prerogative to keep that place happy and clutter-free.*

If a superstition or a belief, or carrying a symbol or wearing a gem stone makes you feel more confident, if it resonates with you, so be it. Do it.

If you genuinely feel following some of these has worked for you and you feel faith in them, do it even if nobody supports the idea. Remember, a stone picked up and worn with faith can have a more positive impact, than what you might wear without faith only because someone says so.

So, what works for you can be distinct. You are unique and what works for you, fulfils you, and makes you feel protected, safe and confident is unique too.

From the Support Toolkit
Good Luck Diary

Observe Good Luck that comes your way though. When things happen - even small things - mark them. Keep a ***Good Luck Diary*** where you can enter things that happen and make you feel lucky. They can be small everyday things too. The more you acknowledge good luck, the more you practice gratitude, the more of it you will experience in your life. To this rule, there is no exception!

If you want to go a step further, then tally your Good Luck at the end of each month.

Practice gratitude. This is an excellent morning task that you can add to your daily routine.

Chapter 2.7
Are You Dimming Your Light?

"I want to come back as the Person I could have been and Never Was."

Remember the time you got a prize at school and realized your best friend had flunked in class? Remember that feeling inside where you wanted to just withdraw into a shell and disappear? Where, although you felt happy inside, you almost did everything you could to mask and hide it. A Sense of guilt was as intense as the happy part. *That was you dimming your light to avoid shining brighter than someone else.*

As vain as it might sound, each of us has experienced the burden of being "better" some time in our life. At a skill, or for being the popular one, the brighter one, the smarter one, the kinder one, the more liked one, the more confident one, the one who scaled great grades at school, the one who flunked but was the most socially active child. We all most certainly have a superlative. Just each may be different. When your area of superlative is in the spotlight and you are shining bright, have you suddenly realised that voice inside which says "xxx is feeling neglected, so let me tone myself down?"

How is that playing up in your life and where you are at?

Maybe because you don't want to make someone else feel slighted. Or because as a child, you saw your mother getting anxious when you got a lot of compliments for your brilliance while your sibling watched quietly.

Kids are magic. They have all the sensory superpowers and their intuitive abilities are much stronger than us adults. Kids will pick up the energy much faster than we would. So, when a parent looks uncomfortable at one child outshining the other, they would catch it, and in a bid to make that parent more comfortable often, they dim their light. This is so subtle that neither the child nor the parent would realise it. After all, it is not a conscious effort to do this.

This forms a habit of dimming our light for others. We can be embarrassed about having more, achieving more or being quicker than those around us to succeed at things we attempt.

Another corollary can be the habit of seeking validation from others. Over time, we stop looking at just our parents but also at the world at large to acknowledge us and appreciate us in order to feel our worth.

As if asking the universe "is it okay for me to shine now?" with no visible answer in sight. This can lead to lower self-esteem, seeking approval from others for every decision and even the fear to make important decisions by ourselves.

You have the permission to Shine! Where and in which area have you dimmed your light? Do you think doing something takes you away from your family tradition or it might be letting a parent or a loved one down who isn't around anymore?

For many who have lost loved ones, the desire to enjoy certain things can be compromised for a long time. Especially, if the person you lost had that desire and it was left unfulfilled. There may be an emotion of guilt that comes up, making you feel like you are letting them down.

Whom are you scared of letting down?

When I started doing this work more intensely, I began to realise how over the years I have dimmed my light time and again to accommodate and make space for others. I am a communicative person; I laugh easily and usually, I am in very high energy. So, it is difficult for others [or even myself] to catch that I am keeping myself small or that there might be any impact inside. Over the years, I have realised several hobbies I didn't pursue because I didn't want to outshine someone close to me, someone I loved.

I have been a guitar enthusiast since childhood. I bought one when I was in school out of my savings. At one point in college, I was dating this person who was so fascinated with the guitar and was a really good player too. It was a time I wanted to pursue the instrument. I never gave it much thought, dropped the idea and moved on. It wasn't until years later that I realised, looking back that the reason to drop it and never get started was the fear of getting better at it and leaving someone who mattered to me behind. And I wasn't even in love!

The truth is maybe, it would never have happened. Maybe, I wouldn't get better, maybe even if I did, it wouldn't matter. But the fear was inside me.

And let's not confuse this with sacrifice or doing it for someone else. Most of the time, we don't even realise we have done this. So, there is nothing glorious about it. There is the reverse situation too. Someone else who is dimming their light for you! Maybe, your partner or a sibling or a parent or a friend. Someone who has a superlative which they see you struggle with, and they dim their light so that you don't feel small. Maybe, you won't, maybe they will inspire you, maybe you will be able to take their help once you see they're superlative. But unknowingly, it is their bid to protect you.

Being observant of when we are becoming the cause of someone else dimming their light for us, is the other side of the same coin. When we help others shine, when we stop them from dimming their light (especially when we are the cause). It is a way to re-ignite our light too.

Why Does Identifying This Matter?

Dimming our light or being fearful of letting someone we love down is a cyclical pattern. Over the years, we get so accustomed to it that we stop realizing when we do it. This can be even stronger for people who are surrounded by loved ones who are not doing as well in their careers or are bickering about what they can't afford or those who are less fortunate in love or life.

Over time, it affects our ability to receive. Receiving is a reflection of self-worth. When we don't receive things easily, we doubt that we deserve them at all. This is a spiral that is difficult to break. It impacts not only money but the way we handle our relationships, or even our health.

Once we keep ourselves aware of this, we are able to release this feeling. We are able to spot when we are doing this to keep ourselves small so that we don't hurt someone or leave someone we love behind.

Work Sheet [Are You Dimming Your Light? Who are You Scared of Letting Down?]

1. Write down three memories from early childhood where you remember being asked to stay quiet when you had something to say or to not share a victory or when something you achieved wasn't appreciated.
2. Write three memories of when friends or siblings or others showed their jealousy towards you and pulled away.
3. Add three more from your teen years or from your first few relationships outside your family [friends, peers at school or college, your date, partner, etc.]
4. Against each of these, write what you did in these situations. Remember to give it time. Close your eyes and relive the memory as much as you can in detail. What did you feel? What did you do when you realised this or were told this? Connect with or identify that emotion.

5. Consciously release those emotions. As an adult, just know that you have every right to always shine the brightest that you can. And that you will never be responsible for overpowering anyone else's light. Remember there is enough in the universe for each of us to shine and you do not have to dim your light to make place for anyone.

Conversation With Yourself

- Am I standing in my own way?
- What is the worst that can happen if I let my light shine?
- Can I let this go after my discovery in the worksheet?
- You have the permission to shine!

Affirmations

- It is safe for me to let my light shine bright.
- It is safe for me to claim my place in the limelight.
- I deserve to be myself and it is safe for me to be myself.

Chapter 2.8

Your 12 Point Support Toolkit

Before we switch over to the other side and work on practical, prudent and logical ways to anchor whatever we have discovered from our Mindset Work, I am leaving you with a few more tools for the Support Toolkit. At the end of each chapter, I have already shared processes and techniques out of your complete Support Toolkit. Here are some more.

You can pick and try many or all of the tools in the kit (here and from the chapters), and pick what serves you the best – what resonates with you and helps you process what you are working with. The tools can be used as a combination for mindset work, and it is not necessary to use every tool for a specific purpose. They all synergize to bring about the desired change.

1. **{Jar of Goodness}**

   - Get yourself a transparent glass jar with a lid. Place it inside your cupboard or on your work table or somewhere that you are likely to see it daily.
   - Whenever you have a win, the smallest thing that brings you joy or a happy moment, put a coin in this jar. It doesn't matter how big or small the coin denomination is. It is symbolic. It also doesn't

matter how big or small the joy or happy moment is, put a coin for every little thing you can.

- Prompts or ideas to when you might put a coin ~ Getting in touch with someone after a long time and enjoying a conversation, working out, spending time with someone you love, finding money when cleaning up, enjoying music or a movie or a hobby today, good news at work or home, being told "I love you," you telling someone you love them, a patch up conversation or a long drive. Don't miss out on these small moments. Put a coin for anything like this! Of course, a coin for every larger win as well.
- At the end of the month or quarter – you can decide how frequently you want to do it – put all these coins together and exchange them for currency. Donate the entire amount to a charity. It doesn't matter how big or small the amount works out to be. Do this in the spirit of appreciating how fortunate you are. And how once you receive your fortunes, you also give back to the universe what you get from it in the faith that it shall come back to you multi-fold!

2. {**Gratitude Journal**}

- Maintain a Gratitude Journal. Not on your laptop or phone, but on paper.
- There is an innate power when we write by hand and express something. It wires whatever we are writing deeper into our brains. Science also

explains this theory under the concept of brain studies. You might like to refer to "Breaking the Habit of Being Yourself," by Dr Joe Dispenza if this subject is of academic interest to you.

- Every night, before you sleep, write three things you are grateful for today. These may be things that happened the same day or from the past, or facts of your life that you are feeling grateful for.
- It is of much more relevance if you delve a bit deeper into your mind and not repeat the same larger things you are grateful for every day. Make an effort to look for the new, small and relevant things for that day. This way, you can develop an attitude of gratitude and attract a lot more of the good things in life by simply being open and aware of receiving.

3. {**Daily Rituals ~ Bookends**}

- Keeping yourself aware all day might be a difficult task, work on the bookends as I call them. The start and the end of the day.
- Create a morning routine that you will stick to, no matter where you are or what time you wake up. Holidays, work travel, vacations, on the other end of the world. Wherever. Whenever. Ideally, this must be a 45-minute routine which works like warming up to get into the day ready for it.
- **Morning Routine Suggestions** – When you wake up, even before you get out of your bed, think of

three things you are grateful for. Make your own bed once you get up. Listen to or read something that is inspiring and adds value to your day. This can be business related or a personal self-development audio/read. Keep about 15 minutes for this. Meditate for 10-12 minutes to anchor in the morning positivity and whatever you have read. Set aside 10 minutes to write down your most important three tasks to finish in the day.

- Until you finish this morning routine, do NOT access your emails, or messages on phone, etc. Keep everything on the "Do Not Disturb" mode so that the notifications are put off. If you are a morning person and prefer working out in the morning, that workout routine is to be done outside of this bookend routine. Ideally, you can finish this bookend, then complete your workout before you get ready to head out for the day!

- **Night Routine Suggestions** - The other bookend would be to close out the night with a daily routine too. Take stock of what you did in the day. Write out your gratitude journal. Do some breathwork or meditate for about 10 minutes. Put all the gadgets in "Do Not Disturb" mode. Ideally, keep your mobile phone, tablets, etc., away from you when you sleep and not at your bedside.

4. **{Journaling}**

   - I don't want to ask you to squeeze too much into your daily routine creating more of a jam.

Journaling is something you can do like EFT, when you feel overwhelmed or feel the need to release something inside.

- There is no perfect way to journal or any desired time. Just maintain a book that you can pick up and journal when you need to empty your mind and headspace to create space for better things.
- Do not go back and read your journaled content often. In fact, you might also choose to never read it and destroy whatever you write from time to time.
- Journaling is a personal tool for you to write down, unedited words that pour out. When you are in the grip of an emotion, or a memory, or anything playing strong on your mind. You don't need to think, or be diplomatic, or plan your words. Nobody is going to read it, not even you.

5. {**Work Out**}

- Physical activity in any format helps in bringing about a sense of balance and natural de-stressing. Workouts in the form of walking, running, cycling, yoga, swimming or any other also promotes better health. Ideally, at least a mild form of exercise must be included in your daily routine. 15 minutes minimum.
- If you are in stressful situations due to work or home or anything else, then you must additionally include in your schedule, at least 45 minutes of work out thrice a week.

- Movement can improve circulation, thus increasing energy levels and also increasing the emotional frequency indirectly. Make movement in some form a part of your routine.

6. {**Meditation**}

- Meditation has gained mainstream importance in the last few years, but it is an ancient technique and can be practised in several different ways.
- The idea of meditation is to be able to de-concentrate and diffuse your mind during the process – to have a clearer perspective when you come out of it. The method you use to diffuse can be a "Mantra" or a chant which keeps your mind coming back to it. It can also be breathwork in a pattern, followed by just sitting with your eyes closed. Open-eye meditation also has gained popularity lately.
- Guided Meditations are available online and might be a good way to get started.
- It is observed that meditating for 10 minutes can actually give deep rest to the body, mind and soul and equates to almost an hour of sleep.
- Suggested Links:
    1. Refer to "What was that Dream?"
    2. Abhyaasa App
    3. https://www.youtube.com/channel/UCbB-ZFJDnWCndDepuoa9_HQ

4. https://www.youtube.com/user/HealYourLife

7. **{Good Luck Diary}**

Refer to "The Karma Angle"

8. **{EFT [Emotional Freedom Technique]}**

Refer to "Releasing Money Emotions".

9. **{The Reframe Exercise}**

Refer to "Reframing Money Stories".

10. **{Scripting}**

Refer to "Reframing Money Stories"

11. **{Forgiveness ~ Ho'oponopono}**

Refer to "Healing Money Memories".

12. **{Sudarshan Kriya}**

- Sudarshan Kriya is a structured breathwork package that includes *Pranayams* [ancient breathing techniques originating from Yoga] and rhythmic breathing cycles. It is known to detoxify the system and help in achieving a complete system reboot.
- Scientific Research on Sudarshan Kriya observes and documents tangible and measurable benefits on the body and mind. Some of the benefits include enhanced immunity, better health, personality development, mindfulness, stress elimination, increased productivity and more.

- After getting trained in Sudarshan Kriya practice, you can do this daily practice at home. The workshops typically take from 8 to 12 hours spread over 3 to 6 days.
- Patented with the Art of Living, Sudarshan Kriya [SKY] is rhythmic breathwork that is taught through in-person and online platforms globally.
- I learnt the Sudarshan Kriya when I was 25 and have been a regular practitioner ever since. It has been a transformational tool in my life that I use to get ready for what lies ahead of me every day.

If you would like to know more, you can connect with @ godluvsfun

Now that you have done layer after layer and worked on unearthing things from the past, (if you have given your 100% to the work so far) you have most likely been able to bring out memories and stories from the past that were holding you back. Perhaps, you got in touch with the emotion that keeps you down time and again and also the beliefs within which you were trying to make everything fit. There is an equal chance that you are bored of it and don't really know if it will work. So, you want to jump to part two straight away.

There are no rules and you can use the book the way it serves you. However, I do believe that we can't fill our lives and minds with great things until we de-clutter the negative and make way for the good.

So, I presume you are now more aware. You have done some of the techniques to process much of the information that you collected. Maybe, you feel more in connection with yourself than before. But for many, this can also be a difficult time where you may feel lost, like you really didn't need to know much of this. It was going fine, things were working well, and this unearthing has actually brought up a lot of negative stuff that you did not even want to remember.

Yes, I get that. That is a natural outcome of all the inner work anyone ever does. But also, a necessary hurdle to overcome in order to be able to live in our zone of excellence and make the most of our lives.

So, what do you do with all this information? How is this really going to serve you?

You run the processes and select what works best for you. Make some of the practices in the Support Toolkit a part of your daily routine so that you can keep the cup de-cluttered from the negatives.

Now, it is time for you to work on the other side. The more practical, tangible, logic-driven work that you can do in a structured format to fill the cup with things that serve you – that bring you ease for your way forward.

Remember ~ ***You are the magic and it is your time to shine!***

3.
Financial Freedom Plan ~ What's Left

Chapter 3.0

The Power of Why ~ Purpose ~ Ikigai

This is probably the strongest reference point to start this part of the book. The left brain. The component in us which uses logic, structure and lateral thinking to orchestrate efforts and skills and bring about a result.

In part one, we have spoken about and (un)covered the right side which processes the abstract, understands music, arts and creativity, stores our memories and works more around energy than logic.

Ikigai is a Japanese concept that means **your 'reason for being.'** 'Iki' in Japanese means 'life,' and 'gai' describes value or worth. Your *Ikigai* is your life purpose or your bliss. It's what brings you joy and inspires you to get out of bed every day.

Ikigai is a book about this Japanese Philosophy of purpose and finding one's calling. The author has spent considerable time touring this area, meeting people, understanding their lives and sharing their experiences. He documents his findings from this tour and his learnings from the time he spends with them.

The book culminates in the fact that purpose or a calling is everything. That, finding and living one's purpose can create healthy and long lives. Increasing longevity and quality. When the book was launched, it became a bestseller and it still remains on the bestseller racks in most book stores at the moment.

In the wake of Covid 19 and the turmoil it caused around the world, the importance of purpose and of making the most of the time we have here have become more mainstream than ever.

In an earlier chapter, we spoke about a dream that is whispered to us when we are born, and a quick pointer worksheet at the end of the chapter listed some questions you could work with to step closer to what that dream, your purpose or your calling [by whatever name called] might have been. If you have worked on that and have your answers, it's time to pull them out of your notes to build an action plan around them.

This time, we evaluate the dreams you unravelled in the context of making life around them and how you might find ways to blend your calling into your life, to bring the optimal fulfilment that is possible for you to experience.

The Importance of Why

The one common factor that you would find if you brought all the successful millionaires in a room and studied their life charts would, without doubt, be purpose. A clear purpose of wanting to get somewhere and why they want to get there.

Of all the questions we strive to find answers for, 'why' can be the most inspiring. When the why is clear, the 'how' finds its way home.

What is the biggest 'why' in your life?

Whether your life's dream is to be wealthy or successful or to find eternal love, or to be the fittest person you know, or to transform the world, or to touch the lives of others, or start your own business or a blend of many of these. What is your 'why?'

On days that are exhausting and seem like the darkness overwhelms you, what is that purpose that makes you want to get up and pick up the pieces and try again?

Who is the person or what is the situation that inspires you? What is the reason that you think you came into this world?

Your calling appears time and again and makes its way into your realm of vision. If you sit up and take notice, it would have knocked on your door several times already. Dig it out now. If it is not on the fore, look deeper.

I recommend reading Ikigai if you haven't already. It can be a great enabler to introspect and find some answers resting inside.

The Three Point Paradigm

During a trip to the United States two decades ago, still in the final year of my post graduation – the two-month long break where we travelled the lengths and breadths of the Nation that fascinates most I know – I vividly remember the morning my cousin's husband, Chip, drove me to the airport. I was taking a two-day trip to a different city to meet a friend, and Chip offered to drive me to the airport before he left for work.

As we talked about life back home and what I was planning in my career and such, he said something about career and making a living. That has stuck with me over the years. Although it was neither the first nor the last time that I had heard this, somehow on that cold November morning, it seemed to have driven a point home.

He shared what he had read a few days back about most people having three different aspects or career options in life, and he felt they rarely overlapped.

I have thought about this several times over the years, and the more I work with decision makers and business owners this comes to light more and more. How, without this important evaluation and in the absence of a well-informed and thought-of decision, the young get led into career streams [read life] that they don't even know if they really want to get into.

Since the 2000s, transitions have become more commonplace. Engineers moving into the restaurant business [I personally know three], doctors pursuing music, people leaving corporate jobs to get into social services; it's all around us. I believe if there is a single largest contributing factor to this, it has got to be the absence of any thorough evaluation when we first start our career journeys. This results in trial and error, and eventually, finding our calling only when life naturally chides us towards our dreams.

What you love to do [Passion]

We all grew up instinctively drawn to doing things. Some hobbies didn't weather the storm, and as we grew up or got busy and as time fell short, we outgrew them. But some stayed on, we found time to pursue them or, at least, indulge in them on and off and they continued to stay a part of our lives.

What is it that you love to do? Maybe, a hobby or something that makes you happy?

It can be cooking, writing, music, reading, cycling, driving, travel, networking, organising events, art, performing on stage…just about anything.

Or they could be attributes like "I love kids" or "I love luxury" or "I love the good life" or "I want to make a difference" or "If I had all the money in the world, I would only travel."

So, let's get straight to what this question then boils down to!

1. What are the things you like/love to do [List out any number of things that you feel this way about]

   ~ If Time and Money were not a constraint

   ~ Which you are able to do more than 12 hours a day if required.

   ~ That gives you fulfilment. You can be so engrossed that you lose track of time, you can forget to eat or drink, and lose awareness of your surroundings even.

~ Which don't make you feel exhausted even when physically tired.

~ That you know you would enjoy doing for the rest of your life, day in and day out.

2. Pick your Number 1 Choice from the List. Rarely you might find more than one that you feel equally passionate about. In that case, you can pick one more.

3. Break down the one [or two] that you picked in point 2.

It's Most likely that people say things that are more generic when they write the list at point 1. But in point 3, they can break it down. If your passion point on the list was, say cooking.

When you break it down, it can mean much more than just that you like to cook, what else can it mean? Specifically, cooking or things related to that as well? Do you like the cutting, preparation and the cleaning after part too?

Do you like any specific type of cooking or any kind and type as long as it is cooking? Look for conditions or restrictions. Maybe, you love baking more than anything else. Maybe, you are fascinated with the idea of live cooking, which means when you cook up a storm for guests when they can see you do that. Maybe, you like to cook elaborate meals but not the everyday mundane ones.

Or maybe, your love for cooking has more to do with entertaining people, setting a great menu, organising the ingredients, setting the table and plating. But if you have hands to help, who can do the actual cooking, that works well for you too.

So, you get the point about breaking it down. Chunk it down as much as you can.

When we look at the whole, we are often unable to see the smaller details that are the real deal makers for us. Look for those. Look for that non-negotiable part in the deal that you absolutely want to have in order to feel it's worth it.

What you are good at doing [Skill]

Independent of what you found in the section before this, what do you think you are good at? This is not in the context of whether you can make a career in it or not, or how long you can do it, or if you like it or not.

What are you good at? What is a skill you know you possess, which has time and again shown up to you and others? What is the skill that makes you unique and assists you to stand apart from others? It may be something you have often received compliments for and deep down you know you can do it well.

It can range from almost the same things as in the first section of this exercise. It can also be playing an instrument, a sport, speaking, writing and composing. Maybe, you have a high IQ, you learn things quickly, you are good at imparting knowledge to others, or maybe you are great in front of the camera. You could be good with ideation or strategy.

This is probably the easiest part to identify. Most of us know this instinctively since we would have had the experience of this since childhood. What we are inherently good at starts showing up early in life. At 5 or 6 years of age, it is already showing up in our actions and behaviours. Adults, at school and home, are quick to catch it. So, we receive feedback on it early too. Once we realize that, we become more observant and are able to even hone these skills to a certain extent knowingly and unknowingly.

If you make a list of five such skills that you possess in varying degrees, which one skill stands out? Here, you can definitely have more than one. For example, you might be someone who is very good at dancing and someone who is very good at imparting information to others too. Alongside, you may be comfortable on camera as well.

This section can have any number of skills and usually, you can find different aspects to these. A fair set of prompts you can use to explore these might be:

1. **What are your personal ability-related skills** ~ Speaking, Observing, Listening, Teaching, Dancing, Singing, any form of Art, Acting – anything that is a talent and you have it in you, which may need honing of course.

2. **In terms of your mental abilities** ~ IQ level, ability to ideate or strategize, logic, setting structure, orchestrating parts into a whole, technical or academic performance.

3. **Social Skills** ~ Introvert or extrovert, ability to fit into different kinds of crowds easily, good

or not at networking, ability to build and retain relationships, comfortable in a crowd you don't belong to.

4. **Business Skills** ~ Are you a leader or team player? Are you effort oriented or result-oriented? Are you a need-a-lot-of-breaks category or a workaholic?

5. **Are you** a seller, planner, producer, orchestrator, people's person, money management focused, trader, exporter, procurement person, etc.? What is that bolt in the machinery of business that you like most to drive/lead?

These skills or personal attributes are an innate part of us, and trying to change these or work against these often leads to burn outs and resentment towards ourselves and everyone else we think we need to compromise these for. It's a great way to find our skill sets and our zones of performance and work around them so that we can get a step closer to our ideal life.

What can make you the Money you want [Lucrative]

An independent introspection about what is the most lucrative thing you can do. Also, for many, the most elusive one. So many people around us are running faster, gasping to get that deadline, that transport, this job, that appraisal or struggling in business to reach that "one day" when they would have made all the money they want so that they can finally start living their lives.

Don't be one of them!

There are several ways people make careers and money. Like I repeatedly say in earlier chapters, the secret is to keep your emotions out of money. There is another too. Don't let money be the deciding factor in how you lead your life or relationships. Money is the greatest resource you can have to make things smoother, but it is not the end and can't be the goal either. Remembering that in critical decision-making will help you to always keep your priorities right.

Some prompts to explore what might be lucrative *for you:* [something that works for one might not for the other]

1. Are you a good salesperson with marketing strategies or plans that you can whip out?
2. Do corporate positions allure you, and do you have the academic backing [or plan to get it] to secure a high-paying corporate role?
3. Are you a designer, artist, or creative person who can perform to an audience?
4. Do you work well in being a facilitator, communicator and do agency roles appeal to you?
5. Are you a behind-the-scenes person who prefers to work on documentation, drafting, and negotiations but leave the front end to others?
6. Do you enjoy paperwork and desk-dedicated roles or meeting people and being on the move?

The fact that you have picked this book and have come this far already tells me that the life you are living is not the life you want to live. You don't want to chase a mirage or run in a direction not knowing where it leads if you can find a better, happier, fulfilling way to get to where you want to go instead.

You are a star yet to shine, in the process now of designing your dream life!

Let's jump right into this. So, you have been hearing about how A or X got rich, the business they do, the product they sell or how they were 'clever' enough to make the most of every opportunity along the way. And you decide one day to replicate what A does. You find out all about it and do your research and jump right into it. You also take some home funds to get started and have an optimistic business plan.

But then, you realise things are not falling in place. Things you thought easy seem like a burden for you to bring about. You are sure it wasn't supposed to be this tough but can't seem to find a way out of it. Costs continue, revenues don't even really start, and before you can get a grip of the situation, the gaps in the cash flow keep growing.

Was the business you chose wrong?

No, it is what others have made money with.

Was it that you didn't work hard enough?

You know you have been putting in 16 hours a day, much more than you planned initially.

What then might be the problem?

Finding where the three overlap can be the key solution and your best life plan to keep it going and growing.

Had you evaluated your passion and your skill sets and then brought about options in that context - proceeded with the business plan and moved on to implementation - the chances of success would have gone up by a whopping 75%.

I attribute 50% of any success to passion, another 25% to skills that can blend to bring forth that passion to your market segment. The remaining 25% only might come from how lucrative a business appears when others are doing it or when you read success stories!

Let's get this three-point exercise done so that we are ready to deep dive into our next level to start putting it all together!

Time to unveil the magic that is you!

Chapter 3.1

Goal Setting ~ Building the Road Map

Picture this. You plan a road trip in the summers. You talk to your family about it and let them know you are making a plan with friends. You then form a group of four who are all equally excited about the trip. You have got the car serviced, all four of you drive and have valid licenses, and have already planned how you are going to divide time to avoid exhaustion.

So, on the scheduled day, you get into the car, pick up the others from the pre-decided meeting points and set out on your journey. You run a checklist to make sure you are stocked up on water and snacks and your mom even packed *chai* in a thermos for you! You are all set. The shades, head gear, everything in. Checklist done and it's time to leave.

As you get into the driving seat first, you instinctively take the route out of your city onto the State Highway that leads to the National Highway about 10 minutes ahead. As you chat and crack lame jokes about your college days, and just 2 minutes away from the National Highway junction, you ask the others about which turn to make! There are three routes at the upcoming junction. One takes you down south cross country, the other crosses over to the east-west bandwidth, and the third takes you up north.

As you realise a sharp sudden silence, you bring the car to a screeching halt and turn back to find everyone with blank faces. Has this happened to you? Have you done all of this preparation, taken days off from work, packed and planned everything, fuelled up, only to then find that not one of you thought of where you want to go?

Then, why would you do it with your life?

I have often wondered why goal setting was not a subject in my formative years, but then, none of the other life skills was either. Our education system, around the world, is not aimed at creating well-informed and aware individuals; it is aimed at creating individuals with degrees who most likely believe that life's goal is to get a secure job and provide for the people they love.

In this entire back-to-back journey of degrees and examinations, I wonder if we stop to learn what might really matter. Breaking down goals and being aware of them comes as the most obvious way to get there, right? At least, the most logical start. It is so natural to understand at this moment as you read this that if you don't know where you want to be 1 year, 5 years or 10 years from now, it is likely you are not getting there unless by accident.

Good goals or bad goals, long and short term, permanent and temporary, knowing where you desire to go is an excellent point to get started!

Let's take a quick look at why goals are important, how they can be instrumental in prodding you forward to being wealthy and having a happy life, and why the absence of clear goals can sometimes let a lifetime pass by without knowing what exactly happened!

In the earlier chapter, we worked on three aspects and finding the overlap for you. This is unique to almost every person. Once you have an idea of what you are passionate about – what skills you have at your disposal given this context and what might be lucrative for you – the next logical step is to build your unique road map.

Important Note for You. *Let me reiterate that none of these exercises is to encourage you to give up an existing vocation or income source to pursue these. It is to start with finding where everything blends and begin as a side hustle. To slowly build things up to be ready for the big plunge. At this point, this is work you do to gain more clarity and preparedness to be ready for this leap.*

The Leap of Faith needs preparation, the parachute, supplies, training, mental strength, a team that works behind the scenes and clarity of mind with a goal to achieve. Faith is the final strike that makes it happen!

Goals ~ Things to Keep in Mind

Clear & Articulate. Imagine if you called to place an order. When asked, you answered vaguely with "Send me anything that is spicy and full of vegetables." What do you think the listener would make of it? What do you think the listener *could* make of it?

We often set out with vague and unclear goals and targets, thinking we will "figure them out" along the way. Like the road trip analogy, starting without a plan gets us nowhere. And moving in the wrong direction is more damaging than sitting in one place.

Your road map and its milestones need to be clear and articulate. If it is to make money, then how much? If it is to get fitter, then what is your target weight? If it is about success in business, what is your definition of success? If you want to become a singer, how can you clearly break this down into a goal? Getting an opportunity to perform live? Getting a playback or recording job? What is it?

For whatever your goals might be and for what your unique definition of success is, get clear about it. And then, put that as your destination on your road map. Then, work backwards from there to find all the milestones – the smaller steps you need to take in order to get from where you are to where you want to be.

Time Bound. Clear and articulate goals also need a timeline. Once you know what your goal post is, and where you are at, mark out your timeline for the entire ride. That gives you clear ends within which to mark out your time-bound milestones.

So, if you are writing a book and say you need to have your book published six months from now. Then, given the time the publishers would take, do some reverse calculations so it's clear that you must have your manuscript ready in four months! Now, it's much easier for you to break down your writing since you know you have four months in hand for the 'x' number of chapters you intend to write!

Also, goals and destinations are never linear. Don't wait to achieve something in one area of your life in order to focus on the other. Although I focus on conversations around wealth, money and success all through this book, I have repeatedly brought about the fact that health and relationships play as important a role. They are just not my areas of expertise!

So, if you are setting a goal for your wealth creation or success in your job and you also want to take a long due family vacation, plan that in. If you want to get fitter to run the marathon next year, plan that in too.

Balance is everything. And goals and life both are not linear, things will happen parallelly and the more you train yourself to multitask and work concurrently on different aspects, the more you will excel in life.

Trackable and Measurable. Do you know what purpose the milestones on highways [and now google maps] serve? They keep us on track; they keep us encouraged. Every milestone reminds us of how far we have come and how much we still have to cover.

Without these, we would not really know about the progress we are making or about how much we have to re-adjust our speed and time to get to our goal post. Of course, we would also totally miss the exhilaration of arriving at the post and being able to celebrate a win.

Keep your final goal and every milestone along the way measurable and find a way to track it. For clear and articulate goals, this is easy to do. So, the question to ask when you first plan your route and road map is, if every step along the way is also measurable and tangible. Abstract goals like "I want to complete my book quickly" do not hold you up for your performance!

Agile. It's a question that has already popped into your mind when reading both the points above, I am sure. "What if my goals change? What if I realise midway that I want something different?"

That can happen more often than not. And when that does happen, you hit the pause button, re-assess and build a new route. We do detours in travel too, right? They are bound to happen in life. But be sure that it is a well-informed change of goal – an empowered decision you are making and that the change is not just a whim because you saw someone else do "that!"

If you have done all the work in the first part of the book and the three-point paradigm system, then rarely would you come across a point where you need a drastic change of destination. Yes, there could be small tweaks where you find different route options or a point where you want to sit down and rest or get a new co-traveller along and slightly change something in the goal. These are small tweaks and will happen several times along the way. Factor them in; it's always good to improvise your plan and keep making it better.

But when you have a doubt and feel the urge to make a complete change, take a break. Just pause and think for at least 72 hours. In these 72 hours, let everything be status quo. And make sure it is not cold feet you are getting!

Sometimes, for many of us, we have been so used to living life the way it was dished out to us that taking charge and charting our own path seems difficult. It is possible to get a feeling, time and again, that you might screw it all up and make a mess. The fear that you might, in fact, land yourself in a situation worse than where you started out. Become aware of this feeling so that you don't give in to it.

The fear of going wrong, and the "what-ifs" will come up no matter which path you take. This is also a way nature gives you a self-check system on auto pilot. But use it only to that extent to keep a self-check and stay on the journey you have decided to chart out for yourself.

Left or Right Brain. When you set out to build your road map, the one question that will keep coming up to you is which side of the function is more important. Goal setting and practically holding yourself to the planned route or inner work so that your mindset is constantly refreshed and new.

The answer is both. Achieving goals, finding success and becoming the version of yourself that you dream of is work that deserves giving it your all. The mindset work is something you will have to keep going back to constantly. And every time you work with any of the worksheets, new answers will come up even to the same questions. This is the work we do constantly. Layer by layer. Every time you feel like you are losing track, go back to these worksheets and find some new things to unearth!

Being positive and having an abundant mindset is a must, but being real enough to understand the risks and finding ways to cross around and beyond them are important things you have to learn. People who tend to be too positive and optimistic often miss crucial facts and perspectives when they create their road maps. They miss unexpected twists and roadblocks that a discerning mind would have seen, putting the left brain to use.

Smart Goals

The magic of goal setting is in the details.

Imagine calling your closest pizza chain and ordering "send me the best pizza you have."

Setting goals like I want to be happier, richer and slimmer are like ordering the universe and your mind in this fashion. "Give me more money" doesn't wire your brain to quantify what exactly you are asking for.

Goals work in two ways. In the first, it is to let out an intention in the universe. The law of attraction or the power of manifestation. Whatever name you call it by, it is the energy perspective of what works for you.

The other, the more structured format is how our goals impact our brains and our efforts. Psychologists affirm that when we focus on one perspective and accept it as our reality, we build muscle memory to work towards that. Our brains build neurons and new habits begin to form. And as we exercise these new habits, they get more and more engrained in our system.

So, when you set a clear goal and write it down, it works at different levels to transform the goal into a reality.

Quick Way to Start

1. Write down five things that you have achieved/ done that you are proud of.
2. What do you want in the next 10 Years? [Write lightly. Not what you can have. Not what you can afford. Just what you want. If everything fell in place, if anything was possible, then what do you want in the next 10 years?] *List 50 things at least. What do you want to have, be, do, hear, see? Health, benevolence, investments, people you want to meet, the person you want to become.*
3. Put a number against each of the 50 things you wrote. The number indicates the number of years you think it might take to get this ranging from 1 to 10.

Out of the entire list, mark out a minimum of 5 items which you can achieve in one year. These are your **Confidence Goals.** The one-year pushed-up goals will pump you up for the long haul. Whenever you have wins and you recognize and celebrate them, confidence gets wired into your system.

People who you meet that are high on confidence know how to use this to their advantage. They fit into their daily routines several small goals and targets that they want to achieve. Adding one round today on the morning run, doing one extra set at the gym, saying no to that one sweet craving today. Making that one recovery call that you are so tempted to avoid and put for tomorrow. Sending out that one proposal that is taking so long to complete. Doing that one difficult conversation with a team member.

Confidence is about energy. Energy doesn't care about the size of the goal, big or small. Every win is a win and it builds a little more muscle memory around your confidence bundle.

This is one of the reasons why the doers, the executors, are often much higher in confidence as compared to the thinkers. Although the value both bring may be the same, the goals are smaller and immediate. The doers are in the habit of making every step measurable. So, every day, they might have several wins! And as they do this, each win is wiring their confidence in. The thinkers usually tend to set goals around more "valuable" things. They don't count small wins. To a thinker, an extra set at the gym is not a goal, and thus, there is no win!

Path of Least Resistance

Rags to riches is a romanticised form of storytelling that we all have read and heard over the years. These are fascinating stories, and on one hand, they can be inspiring since the moral it communicates is that anyone can be rich or successful or healthy.

On the other, what it fails to narrate though is, that making money, retaining it, managing it well and exponentially growing it can be easy too. It doesn't always have to be a struggle that holds you back or keeps you down. The right information, the ability to take good decisions, and financial education can all be keys to creating the wealth you desire with ease.

The other problem with glorifying struggle is that people who don't have enough of it in their lives are put into the lucky box. Their struggles of a different kind are not acknowledged. I am on the other side of the fence. I have had almost everything easy. Wealth; because I was a millionaire at 17. Love; because it came into my life like fresh breeze at the most unexpected yet perfect time. Access to social networks and even building connections with people.

But I had my struggles. With early trauma and subtle PTSD which has continued over the years due to childhood experiences. The formative 6 years of my life have weighed in heavily on the remaining 40. And it's only in the last 4 years that I have been able to take charge and make substantive changes.

With all of this tucked away inside, I had bitten the *Positivity Pill* a long time ago, and so, life continued to be smooth and easy.

Learn to find the path of least resistance whenever you chart your road map. How can you make it easier, how can you increase the metabolism, convert the max of the input into your desired output? How can you put in 1 unit to create a result of 10 units? If you are someone who looks for the complicated way, you are going to find only those. If you think success is a mirage, or money is difficult, that is going to become your financial reality sooner or later.

They say, "Hire lazy people; they find the easiest way to do everything!"

Are you the "Status Quo" person? Basically, the one who lets things be how they are until someone else comes and moves them. The attitude of "anything will do" often brings us just that - anything!

Being assertive and clear on what you don't want is as important as having clarity on what you do want.

5 Most Common Goal Setting Mistakes

- ***Being the Big Thinker***

  If you start out with illusions of grandeur, you'll likely never start, or you will mess it up. Sir Richard Branson's group owns and runs 400 businesses under their flagship with more than 50,000 employees worldwide. But he has said in an interview that 40 years ago if they had started with this goal, they would most likely have messed up and never made it.

  Why? Because you will overestimate your sales, you will overbuild and overspend on the perfect systems even before you start out. While you are dreaming of your contribution to society, you will most likely miss the payroll for your team!

Learn to start small. Start where you are. Build a plan, start moving today, evaluate and improve. Loop.

On a day-to-day, practical basis, thinking too big puts you in a state of analysis paralysis and keeps you from doing anything at all. When you figure that your product or service isn't revolutionary yet or you're not changing the world, you have a convenient excuse to wait, delay, and continue to plan, plan, and plan some more rather than work, work, work.

You've heard it before, "The journey of a thousand miles begins with a single step." Think small. Think about today's step. Then, with each step you take, work on growing and getting better. In due time, you will realize you're much further along than you could have even imagined when you first started. You might even travel so far in your constant and never-ending day-to-day growth and improvement that you might actually exceed your initial goals!

- ***Being like your father or mother***

As you set your goals, look at which of them really belong to you. Is there something your father or mother always wanted to do and couldn't get to do? Something you heard growing up to be the ultimate goal anyone can have? Be wary of picking up dreams and goals from the ones you love.

More often than not, you won't even realize when your goals get "inspired" by those in your closest circle. The line between what was their dream and what is yours blurs.

On the practical side, technology has reached several tipping points. We are the only humans who have lived through the transition from a state of linear progression into the space of exponential growth.

Ray Kurzweil describes this phenomenon in his essay, "The Law of Accelerating Returns." He says, "We won't experience 100 years of progress in the 21st century – it will be more like 20,000 years of progress (at today's rate)."

Leadership styles and goals set 30 years ago are completely irrelevant today. And that's the minimum time span that has lapsed between how your parents set their goals and how you will be setting yours. Time to step out of the shadow of "how things *were* done" and move into "how things *are* done."

It's your life; set goals that are personal and mean something to you.

- ***Wanting to do it all at Once***

Chunk it down. If there is one thing you must remember, it is this. In goal setting, in delegation, in planning your systems. Chunk it down to the smallest possible denominator.

Goals which are too macro level tend to blur the lines of actually doing the work to getting there. Goals should be set in a way that when you bring them to the smallest detail, you must know what to do today to get closer to your goal. If you can't do that, then, most certainly, you are going to be spending your days with the goal only on paper and never doing anything to productively get towards it.

Every step counts but sitting in a place making your goals grander and better and waiting for something magnanimous to give them meaning is a sure way to delay and procrastinate your goals.

- ***Setting up for Sure-shot Success***

And avoiding failure.

The entire universe is built on duality. Just as you cannot have a day without night, up without down, or good without evil, you cannot have success without failure. It's not possible.

The former President of IBM, Thomas Watson, advises, "The key to success is massive failure."

The only way to accelerate your success is to speed up your failure. The only way to elevate the magnitude of your success is to raise the stakes of your failure. Stop trying to avoid it. Pursue it with passion and joy. When you do fall or fail, celebrate it. You've grown and you've given the duality pendulum a nudge that will have it inevitably swing back on your side.

The only thing holding you back from realizing your potential and accomplishing any goal your mind can stretch to is fear. If you can learn to turn your fear into fun – something you make friends with rather than avoid – your potential will open up and your greatness will shine.

- ***Falling in Love with the Goal***

Love is Blind. When you fall in love with your goal, you can become terribly short-sighted on the real problems it might throw your way. Sometimes, you could miss the obstacles because you have romanticised the goal so much that it becomes more a part of defining who you are rather than the potential it holds.

Keep love out of the equation. Keep it 'No Strings Attached.' I repeatedly say keep the emotions out of all money decisions. So, if you want to achieve something to make your parents or spouse proud of you, or to get even with an ex-business partner who left you midway for a more lucrative offer, or to take revenge on that cousin who has always run you down, think again.

If you have the slightest doubt right now that any of these have crept in, go back to the

3-paradigm exercise! In fact, also go back and do the "Releasing Money Emotions" work again.

You have your purpose in place and you have just set your goals! Let's see how rejection can be a redirection, leading you to new doors. Let's set some paradigms to get into the groove - your rules or framework which sets the pace for your journey ahead - before we get into what might be the most important part of this book for many of you: The Practical Guide and Work along for your Money Management System set up!

"As you move towards your goals, how far you have come is a far better measure of your success rather than how far you still have to go."

Chapter 3.2
Another Door is Opening

"Standing in front of a closed door for too long can make you feel like there's something wrong with you – when the truth is it's just not your door."

– *Nakeia Homer*

Life can take unexpected turns sometimes, and most of the time, your blessings will come disguised as curses. The key is to be able to differentiate and keep doing what you can.

Markets will crash, taxes will go up, economies will slow down, wars in a different country will affect yours, inflation will hit, appraisals might not happen as you expect. You may have a health irritant, you could lose money, you may lose a loved one and you could land up in a break-up.

When we have a plan that goes over decades, some of these things are bound to happen, and they will. There can be several ways when speed bumps will hit and you might face setbacks, small and big, feel like you have gone back a few steps and need to gather yourself and start again. It is in times like those that you might want to come back and do the work again.

You would have new memories and stories to clear, new emotions to deal with and new systems to put in place.

Rejection = Redirection

Picture this. Earlier, you had the car that you and your friends got into for a road trip, remember? Where all of you stocked up and got prepped and everything, only to realize you didn't know where you were going! Now, you know where you want to go. You have the road map ready and you have marked the route out with milestones and halts along the way.

This time, when you set out and are a few hours into your planned route, you realize the car is heating up. So, you need to drive with the windows down and look for the closest fuel station to get it seen. You find one eventually and ask the guy to check the car. He tells you it will take a few hours and it is evening already. The only option you really have is to stay that night in a motel across the road and get the car done. Your car, the hardware, your system broke down. The time it takes to put it in place, the cost to do that and the inconvenience caused to all of you is part of the game. If you have worked on your mindset and have practised the discipline of staying geared, you will spend the night requesting a personal bonfire in the garden, which barely looks visited. You will get up the next morning, treat the motel like an adventure and get back to work.

Along the way, if you have 1000 kilometres to drive to get to your destination, you certainly know there would be points where roads divert; GPS can't catch smaller rural routes, and repair work can cause road blocks. What do you do? Do you drive back home? Do you stay where you are?

Obviously, you find the next best route, use diversions and shortcuts sometimes, and at other times, you may find even longer routes to get to your destination. You know you want to get there. You have a fun trip planned there and you are going to miss it for nothing!

Why Would You Not Do That in Life?

When a door shuts on you, another opens.

If you look back, you will find a pattern in this too. Maybe, you prayed for something which didn't really materialize for you. Today, in hindsight, you realize you are doing far better without it [if you still doubt it, maybe you want to look at your high school crush!]

When you hit a block, when you find your plans on a toss, look deeper. The solution is always attached to the problem. If you zoom out and take a look, do some inner work and get some fresh air, you will find the way to go right through the problem. Face it and get through on the other side.

A plan failing, a business going into losses or even a personal loss you face does not seal your fate. What you make of it does.

When I started writing this book and as it developed from chapter to chapter, I found myself at a threshold several times where I had to decide if to share anecdotes from my own life and those of others, or if it would be better not to get into that zone. But real stories are real. And I know that if I had to share with you my deepest, uncomfortable truths, it was opening up parts of my life, but it could also be a catalyst for you to look into the crevices where some truths still reside.

And here's where we talk about redirection. I probably am opening up the most uncomfortable truth that I am yet to put out in the public domain. 1981, a year of transformation and a complete 180-degree change for me. Some good, some bad. But like I said earlier, some blessings are born out of curses.

1981 – My Year of Transformation ~ A Door finally Closes

It was consistent abuse and trauma that my mom and I faced for 6 to 8 years of our lives. Every day was a battle, every moment was full of fear of being harmed. The noise, the conflict, the uncouth behaviour that she was not accustomed to and didn't want me to be accustomed to either. Our best tools were each other, the fairy tales and books and music and all our conversations about the world, nature and art.

It was a summer afternoon. Schools were shut for the summer holidays and the annual holiday ritual was complete with all the cousins staying over at my maternal uncle's.

But Mom and I were in our room, our little space in the large 3.5 BHK house where 8 others lived with us. It was what I desperately wanted to believe was "home."

My maternal cousin, who worked with a leading Mumbai developer, was to come by with tickets to a movie show. Since she had an access to getting tickets from the cinema quota, she was always able to get us those even when shows were houseful.

My mom wanted to make the payment for the tickets. So, she went to my grandparents' room to ask for some money. The tradition of keeping all my dad's earnings with his father was something neither he nor my mom had objected to since it had been initiated when my dad was still single. In many Indian households, this tradition was still prevalent in those times.

When my grandfather questioned my mom about why she wanted money, she simply answered that my dad had asked her to take it from him. He pressed further on, so she said it was for movie tickets.

These were days when the income was meagre, costs were high, but my dad used to receive a lot of gifts from clients since he worked as a Managing Partner in a renowned CA Firm. Diwali meant boxes of dry fruits and sweets that would come for us, but would invariably make a detour to different rooms before they got to us. By the time the open and half-finished box came to our room, only the sugary sweetened strawberry remained. I guess nobody else in the house liked them either!

That afternoon, as always, my uncle jumped into a conversation that was essentially between my grandfather and my mom. My mom was badass. She was not coy, she was not quiet and she was the one to call a spade a spade. She was educated, talented, intelligent, kind and tolerant. But she wasn't the one to put up with nonsense quietly. When the conversation was getting out of hand, my grandfather refusing to give her the amount, (by the way it was less than 100 Rupees) she suggested he speak to my dad and then do whatever he says. I think that was fair even today in hindsight.

But my uncle was miffed with that. He thought it was disrespectful to my grandfather. So, he jumped in to argue. My mom told him not to get involved since it didn't concern him. That miffed him off further. He pulled her by her arm and abused her.

My mom, in contrast to my dad, came from a very different culture. Financially stable and educated, her father was a lawyer who, post his army posting, used to teach law in IPS [Indian Police Services] Training Schools across the country. She lived in sprawling homes at every posting they had, where integrity, discipline and patriotism were a way of life. Being abused to the face by her younger brother-in-law who was actually living off her was a bit too much. But she pushed him away and simply told him to just stay out of it.

What happened next was shocking. For me, all of 6, it was numbing. I have never before or after that seen anything like that. He pulled my mom by the hair and flung her to the floor. She was wearing a saree, which he pulled, and tore her blouse. He kept abusing her and hitting her. He kicked her incessantly with his shoes on. He was wearing shoes with a block heel. {It's a detour, but I wonder what he was doing with his shoes on since he never went to work!}

My mom, who was five months pregnant, began to bleed.

His wife watched. His parents watched. Later on, the parents confessed that they have never been able to stop him when he got into a rage. This was apparently not his first!

That day, my mom miscarried. Again. It had hit once more where it hurt the most. She had several injuries on her torso, stomach and arms. But, perhaps, the deepest injury was the one of humiliation and the assault on her dignity. During her medical check-up, the mark of the shoe was found by the medical team and was reported to the police.

The denial of trauma can be even worse than the trauma itself. My grandparents and the rest of the paternal family put emotional pressure on my dad, and he, in turn, on my mom to withdraw the case. After four days of resistance from my mom's side of the family, mom gave in to the pressure and signed the documents to withdraw the case. The condition being [I told you my mom was badass!] she wouldn't go back to that house and neither would I, no matter what the outcome. He was free to do what he felt was right.

This uncle got out of the lock-up and wasted no time planning his next "*kaand*" [*Kaand* loosely means 'conspiracy' in Hindi.] Along with a relative, he hatched a plot to kidnap a developer in the area and ask for ransom [this was before extortion became the official term.]

The developer turned out to be smarter and he got them arrested red-handed. He was in the lock-up once again, within a week of his earlier stint. This criminal case against him went on with frequent hearings until 1993. For 12 years. And ashamed of what he had done, his parents decided to announce to the world that this case was related to my mom's "fabricated" complaint.

5th May 1981 was the fateful afternoon when our ordeal happened. 12th May, exactly a week later, was the kidnapping incident for which he eventually got tried.

The humiliation that afternoon was neither the beginning nor the end of the abuse. It was only the peak in terms of physical abuse.

After my mom was discharged from the hospital, we moved to her brother's [my mama's] place. We lived with them for a few years until we were eventually able to get a place of our own.

The way this door closed on us was less than ideal; the assault and the trauma it induced never really went away. My mom probably took that day's insult and humiliation with her, and I continue to process it in some part of me even today.

However, there was a certain redirection. My mom often told me, had that day not happened and the simmering abuse stayed verbal and emotional like it had been all those years, we would have still probably continued to live there in the hope that something someday would change. With no other place to go or a place of our own, it wouldn't have been a decision we would have taken. That nightmare actually shook us out of our slumber. And in the most undesirable way, took us a step closer to our dream life which was waiting around the corner!

That day, on 5th May 1981, as we stepped out the main door and turned back to look at my grandfather who looked like a hapless helpless man, she asked him, "You won't say anything?"

His reply was, "Just leave." At that moment, we knew that the door had closed on us.

But the purpose of this chapter is that there were two doors that opened at the same time; in 1981, on some other side of the country, that were to shape my life in the years to come!

Also 1981 ~ A New Door Opens {Infosys}

Seven determined IT guys began their journey in the early months of 1981 in Bangalore, before it became the city of dreams for IT aspirants!

One of these seven. Nandan, who hails from our community, had an industrialist relative also from our community, who happened to be my dad's first client after he started practice. So, when they got together and were looking for a strong professional team to be onboarded for the journey they were about to begin, this gentleman suggested my dad's name to be their finance go-to person.

After a few calls, an introduction and some follow-up discussions later, my dad was onboarded. The team was looking for someone to be an insider for them, who was well versed in finance, tax and cross-border transactions. Having just begun his practice and unsure of how things would pick up, a stable income was more important for him then as compared to a stakeholder position in what was to become one of the leading IT giants of the country in the coming decades! He joined the team, albeit as the Statutory Auditor and Financial Advisor.

In 1981, Infosys was born. The rest is history.

The small garage that first housed this dream and what this grew into eventually, were two different worlds. Much has been discussed and written about this company over the years, but a handful have had the fortune of watching it so closely. And in my formative years, when we absorb, we see not only through our logic, but as kids, we absorb energy too. I was a curious child, and listening to the elders talk around me always resulted in me having a question-answer session with my mom at night, for terms I hadn't understood. She would do her best to simplify complex content for me to understand it. Bangalore and Infosys became a familiar, informal training grounds for me even before I knew it.

By the time 1984 arrived, every summer, we would spend two months in Bangalore. While dad had work to do and his team was there for the duration, we would be there for our summer stay. So, practically, year-on-year, we continued to spend two months each year in the garden city.

The fact that we had friends, relatives and cousins to hang out with made it a second home for me. By the time I finished school and entered college, I had already had enough exposure to how this company worked, to what their ethics were and how traction was building up.

While the men folk spent long hours creating something valuable, much of the time the families also got together and spent the days, evenings or weekends in and around the city doing different things. Those years gave me a close brush with seeing in person how a garage start-up [the term was not officially up and about then] turned into this global corporation. I was able to visit their offices and could hear from Murty uncle himself about their ethos and passion, and on what basis they had set up most of their systems. I have fond memories of Murty uncle, Sudha aunty and their families.

Aunty's family is one of intellectuals. Her father was a renowned doctor in Southern India, a legacy her sister is taking forward. Her mother – a quintessential Indian grandmother straight out of your imagination – was also a wonderful cook!

Although the relationship came to an end professionally in 1999, when Infosys was listed on NASDAQ and certain global regulations had to be met, the personal connection continues.

When I was 18, I decided I wanted to get trained on the job and experience the corporate world since I was still dabbling with what career I eventually wanted to pursue. By this time, our fortunes had changed multi-fold and we had become the new, reluctant millionaires.

Mom had always been of the opinion that what is in the bank must never mess up our minds, and we essentially stay rooted to our "middle-class" values! For me, that was a way of life. I had seen that in my own home and I had interacted with several people closely by now to have seen and learnt this. So, it came easy to stay in the "think before you spend" bracket or the "don't waste it just because you have" bracket. Role models like the Murtys added to that.

In 1994, I decided to work on Infosys projects as part of the audit team under my dad's firm. Since I had signed up for my articleship already, it was possible to do. It was around the time when the electronics city unit was set up, the first of the many campuses that they now have. The next two years opened my eyes and my exposure to a completely different level. Infosys did it much before anyone did. The campus was like a completely "Employee-Oriented" township, with health clubs, open gardens, cafes and different wings housing each department. What struck me as a progressive HR step was that the card was swiped when you entered the campus and left it. The mental wellness of people was given a lot of importance. In these two years, I learnt world-class systems, policies, details about disclosures and compliance about how businesses were set up and grown, how contracts were closed and how work culture was created.

Remember my superpower that I mention elsewhere? Being a super quick learner! These two years, I believe, contributed to a lot of everything that I started my entrepreneurial journey with!

Although my stint with Infosys started much later and was a short one of learning and getting ready for my leap, for my family, this started in the same year 1981. The year when a door had closed on us, this one had opened. And this was a long stint, forming one of the peaks and important milestones in my dad's professional life. For us as a family, these were the years when we saw a complete turnaround: socially, mentally, emotionally and financially.

And Also 1981 ~ Another Door Opens {Art of Living}

In 1981, a quaint village on the outskirts of Bangalore also saw another different kind of start-up, a spiritual one. While we were here in Mumbai, battling with our own assault, trauma and stress, unsure which way to go. When many five-year-olds [and so many others around the world] were probably fighting battles too large for them to win by themselves. In Udayapura, was a dream being born, of a stress-free world. Although it was to take me 20 long years to be acquainted, I don't think it was a mere coincidence that in the same year, at different corners of the country, two different things were waiting to shape my life!

Today, the International Centre of the Art of Living, nestled in the midst of Greens and an entire township by itself has come far from what it might have looked like in 1981.

I'd had exposure to spirituality early in life. Although my concept of spirituality, like my mom's, has always been about living a certain way, having the right intention and never consciously harming those around you, I was also exposed to traditional spirituality due to my extended family. My aunt, where we lived for three years before moving into our own home, my mami [mother's brother's wife], is a devout person. She spends a lot of her time with God literally. She was an ardent devotee of Sri Satya Sai Baba, a revered saint from Southern India. Whenever He visited Mumbai, it was 4 A.M mornings for us (for me, it was a picnic!) and we were put under the shower, dressed up and taken along with them to pay our respects. A place called Dharmakshetra [meaning the place of Dharma] was their Mumbai headquarters. Along with my cousins, I was also enrolled on the "Bal Vikas" classes, a Sunday morning only-for-kids moral values workshop. With time, this became a habit to follow. Without having to process or think about it too much. As kids, our expectations from life are few. And adjusting those to what we are told to do is easier.

These classes happened at the places of people I was fond of. I played with their kids, and many kids from the colony we stayed in used to attend class. So, the before and after fun was my motivation to land up there on an early Sunday morning!

Although, to this day, I revere the saint and His Organisation, which have done phenomenal work for the society around the globe and run several projects in healthcare and education worth lauding, somehow it didn't resonate with me individually on a spiritual level. Perhaps, I was too young or it was just not my time yet.

Later in the mid-1990s, my parents were led to their Guru, their Spiritual Master. For those unversed, taking a Guru (it's really the Guru taking you as their disciple!) is a common and ancient principle in the Indian culture.

But it's like falling in love, I think! When it happens, it happens! You could look for love all your life and not find it. And it could turn up when you least expect it to!

My dad was appointed to the managing committee of the *Math*, representing our community. For the unversed again, most brahmin communities have a "Math," a structured system that houses their roots, and is led by a "Mathadipati" who is the Spiritual Leader of the community. My dad's tryst with his Guru happened when the Guru ascended to this position in the mid-90s. My mom met the Guru soon after. Both of them were devoted and also had the good fortune of being able to devote their time and energy to the Math and the Guru.

I also got on to their road trips when Mom and Dad travelled as a mix of Math-related work and leisure. This was one week each month. Both Mom and Dad travelled with the Guru to different parts of the country too, and on several occasions, the Guru also visited and stayed at our home in Mumbai. By this time, we had moved to a Mumbai home in Juhu, where we could accommodate all the entourage and other arrangements that accompany the visit or stay of a Spiritual Master.

I had the opportunity to spend a lot of time with the Guru myself and also to have interesting conversations around God, Spirituality and the like. He is intelligent and well-informed, and there is something soothing about His presence. In long conversations and my time spent at the Math during all those visits, the Guru, I believe, played a very important role as a spiritual guide and a campass to my one-on-one tryst with spirituality. Swamiji, as he is called in the community, has left an indelible mark on my life and on my lessons on spirituality.

Personal relationships of any kind depend heavily on communication, access, time spent and the freedom to ask questions. I believe a Guru-Disciple relationship is the most personal relationship there can be. In our ancient traditions, it is believed that a Guru can elevate us, can be the window to spirituality and can even be our gateway to a better afterlife! In that sense, if this were true, it also then means that the Guru is the one with whom, our relationship transcends time and even our lifetimes. What can be more personal than that?

Truth be told; I wasn't really searching for a Guru. I had been a sceptic in these matters. These spiritual trysts only made me more sceptical. I don't like boxes. I call a spade a spade. I am unabashed. And I am not ashamed of it.

In 2001, 20 years after this door had opened somewhere someplace, I was in a transitional period. I had appeared for my final exams and the results were expected. I had a business plan I wanted to pursue. With all my to-be partners backing out at the last minute, I had two weeks on hand and not much to do!

My cousins and some in the family, who had done an Art of Living Workshop, had been recommending it to me. I had also heard about this from friends earlier, almost 4-5 years before this point. But then, as I said earlier, the Guru takes us in when He feels we are ready, I guess.

I found a Public Speaking Workshop of the Indo-American Society which filled up one week, and the other week, I found the six-day Basic Course of the Art of Living to do.

The six days came like a breath of fresh air. The techniques, the Bhajans played, the knowledge points and the interactive sessions were eye-openers for my still-a-bit-sceptical mind. The Sudarshan Kriya, the soul of this beautiful course, opened up things at different levels and I experienced a deep sense of rest [I didn't know then that it was Meditation] during the course.

I wanted to experience that again. The home practice is really simple and I committed to doing it for the 90 days that we were asked to commit to. During the six days of the course, we were asked to abstain from non-vegetarian food and alcohol, both being a part of my social routines. I thought continuing to abstain from it for the 90 days of practice could facilitate me to feel that sense of rest again. So, I stayed away. In fact, as a matter of discipline, for six months after this course, I abstained from onion and garlic too [which I came back to eventually.]

I attended parties, visited people, travelled, and hosted people, but continued to stay away from these and continued with the practice. In these initial 90 days, I had different kinds of miracles, big and small, that were experiential. Things I couldn't explain and others wouldn't understand. Perhaps, this is what spirituality meant.

90 days turned into a "few more months" as people around me wondered what was going on. I realised when you want to break a habit, all you need to do is postpone it. One day or one week or one month at a time. I had attempted to turn vegetarian several times earlier and managed for short spans, eventually getting back to it. This time, it has been 21 years!

Four years into the course, after doing the advanced levels, I decided to attend the training to become a teacher. After going through two vigorous Training Programs, I became a faculty for the course that had begun a transformation in me.

What resonated with me, my deal clincher, was the disciplined and yet free-spirited Guru Sri Sri Ravi Shankarji. Running several social projects around the world, with a network of teachers, service warriors and at all the levels of society one can think of, my personal resonance also came from the fact that Gurudev [or Guruji as He is lovingly called] is always accessible to the millions of followers around the world. When you need Him, you have a way to reach Him.

And no, I don't mean in Meditation. I mean in real!

To get answers to questions, solutions to problems, to just find peace and soothing on difficult days. To get reassurance on days when you doubt yourself.

The other was the absolutely fair system of gender equality. Both men and women are teachers, seva warriors, part of the entourage. Women can become *Swaminis* or *Brahmacharinis*, the way men can become Swamis or *Brahmacharis*.

Upanayana or threading is an ancient technique, where spiritual knowledge is imparted to the receiver and a holy thread to be worn for life is put. Over the centuries, the patriarchal systems that took over discontinued this ritual for women and it was only done for men. Although, the original ancient scriptures suggested it be done for both. In Art of Living, we do upanayana for women too.

The resonance was clear. Gurudev and the organisation are as out of the box as I was; it was a feeling of coming home. This was the spiritual door that had opened for me in 1981. It was like the spiritual culmination that was waiting for me. Perhaps, I was waiting for it too without even knowing it!

If there is a rejection you are facing right now, be sure there is a new direction about to enter your life. It may take time or it may be immediate. But it will make its way to you. Keeping yourself on track, keeping your right and left brain balanced and in sync and giving it your all, is what you can do. You can be ready and keep honing your skills so that when the opportunity knocks, you can open the door!

As we move to the last but crucial part of this book, where you will build your personalised Money Management System, my team and I wish you a great journey ahead, as you set out to transform your Finances and Life!

You are magic, and let the magic shine!

Chapter 3.3

Functioning From the Space of Broke [And Being a Millionaire]

"Do you know why a rocket surges higher than an aeroplane? Because its bum is on fire!"

Daymond John describes his journey in the book "Power of Broke." For a reader, this book is a powerful narration of his tryst with fate and the turnaround he created. As a shark on the Shark Tanks show, what he says has tremendous value. Life gave him little, and so, he was forced to function from a space of broke.

But everyone won't have a rags-to-riches story. Living from the space of broke, or economy, or cost-benefit is a habit we must cultivate if we want to look at the results and correlate them to actions.

Some of us have had it easy. We had wealthy, successful parents or were born into a well-placed family and we probably haven't seen how life can be when you have to manage a month on a budget or have to make a choice between a weekend movie and paying for your monthly tuition. Everything is paid for.

But remember a time when your phone battery was draining out and you had no charger on you? How you switched from calls to messages only and turned off every app that you didn't really need. You may have refrained from playing the online games you are addicted to just so you could save enough charge to make it to the party you had been organizing. Basically, you switched to a Power Save Mode because power, at that time, was scarce.

Or a time you forgot to fuel up when you left in a rush and realised there was no gas station in sight for a long drive. Where you decided not to guzzle fuel, used your best budgeting skills to put the car cooling system on and off to keep you cool and yet, use the least possible fuel? Here you switched to Fuel Save Mode because, at this time, fuel was scarce for you.

That was you functioning from a space of broke! Broke doesn't have to mean a space where there is a lack or no access to what you want to have, it is a space where you can train your mind to make the best use of what is available at hand, to optimise its use and make the best benefit from it that you would otherwise miss.

For most of the world's population, functioning from a space of broke is not a new concept. That's how many families across the world spend the last week of every month. That's how a student on pocket money manages the outings going Dutch. That's how homemakers manage and utilise the limited funds they are given each month, to make sure everything is met, before allocating anything towards luxury.

So, why should we function from a space of broke? Is that not a space of lack? Is it not opposed to the law of attraction?

No.

Even when you can afford better, get into a habit of optimising what you have, knowing mentally that you can have whatever you want. That is functioning from a space of broke [and living like a millionaire.]

Every amount you spend, the time you give, and the energy you invest has an ***Opportunity Cost.*** If you want to become a smart wealth creator and a money magnet, relationship magnet, or health magnet, you have to start to make quick slice decisions around the opportunity cost concept.

Whenever you expend any of the three resources you have, invest them into what can bring you the highest return in terms of whatever that return can be quantified as.

If you are working on your fitness currently and say your goal is to run the next marathon, you can expend the same 2 hours every day doing different kinds of workouts. But in order to optimise your effort-to-goal ratio, you would need to get expert advice and plan your routine so that every hour you expend in the coming months takes you tangibly closer to be fit to run the marathon.

The same applies if the goal is in terms of making a relationship work or taking yourself to the next level financially.

The Three Paradigms to Function From a Space of Broke

1. ***Know that every Resource once used is exhausted.*** Even if you have infinite access to more, that particular unit of the resource is exhausted when used. There is no way you get back that hour spent, that amount gone or that energy expended.

2. ***Know every Resource has multiple options*** of use, choosing any one always means choosing against all the others. Saying 'yes' to one means saying 'no' to all the others.

3. ***Understand the Correlation*** of the input to the output and measure it to see where it is on the graph of what you want to achieve from it.

Pointers to Create the Discipline of Broke

1. Define what Necessity, Premium and Luxury mean to you in every aspect of your life. This helps you to determine the input-output ratio and take slice decisions quickly.

2. Ask yourself if this is investing or spending. Whenever you put in money, time or energy into anything, it is an investment only if it brings you or will bring you the desired output in future and is made without getting your emotions involved in the decision. If emotions are coming in the way, do your EFT.

3. Be an informed spender. Research, get the information about what you are about to put

yourself into and negotiate hard (even when you really, really want it.)

4. Whenever pushed into an immediate decision and in doubt, take 24 hours to decide. (Buy that time, sleep over it, 24 hours is enough time for you to differentiate between impulse/temptation and a well-informed decision.)

Functioning from the space of broke is one of the key elements of money management. If this discipline is developed and followed through, it becomes a habit. And this habit can become an accelerator to multiply and optimise what you make of your life!

Practice in the Space of Broke Until It Becomes a Habit

- *Being Innovative*

  Heard the old adage "Necessity is the mother of invention?" When there is no other way, thinking out of the box becomes the way.

  The most important thing you can do to function from the space of broke and to practise it until it becomes a habit is of being innovative, being resourceful and function out of the box.

  If you can create things that others can't or which look impossible to others, that's an art that can take you a long way.

- *Seek Adventure*

  Adventure can be the cornerstone of functioning from the space of broke. Have you ever thought of how some kids are not happy with anything! They are complaining about the vacation they missed in the holidays while their friends took it. The ones who feel not having shopped for 3 months for luxury clothing is unfair. Or the ones who think not throwing their birthday parties in places that matter is below their standards.

You have surely also seen kids who are happy with the rainwater puddles and playing with puppies on the streets. They have their hands dirty and faces stained with their last fall a few minutes ago, but are back on their feet wrestling for fun with their best buddy. The ones who can still make a boat out of paper and play the simple games that don't run on technology. Who don't have the best running shoes but that doesn't stop them from running the fastest!

You can make your challenges an adventure. Or you can make your challenges your problems. To crib and complain about. When you are having fun, the world seems like a better place. Life seems like a good deal. Once you decide, you can just about have fun everywhere.

- *Luxury Detox each Month/Quarter*

Heard of the technology detox people are talking about? Great idea! In the same way, how about doing one day away from the luxury you are used to, try a day living a life for experience or adherence to just "be able to!"

A luxury detox could look like using the Metro instead of your own car. Or a smaller car compared to your luxury drive. Maybe, you could drive yourself if your driver does it every day. You could eat a street meal or keep away from the luxury gadgets you are used to. One day, each month or each quarter on what suits you better, live a life at least two levels below your means and different from what you are used to. Just being aware and putting yourself in this position can be a huge lesson while also being an effective break from the mundane as well.

The light is neither in your situation nor in the hand life dealt you. The light is in what you make of it and how you let it shine! Shine on!

Chapter 3.4

Setting Up Your Framework ~ Getting into the Groove

Every individual has a blend of ideologies and rules that they swear by. What you are as a person, your ethos, your style and how you like to function, can all determine what you bring to the table. Your unique signature style can become your legacy.

It is unfathomable for me or anyone else to give you these guidelines all at once, but I share some pointers to prod you into thinking along these lines. What is your ideology? How do you like to do things? Are you a non-conformist? What does your dream mean to you?

Read on to just explore and find some answers to start setting your rules for success and growth. They will evolve over time; some you may never have even thought of. Just read this chapter like a free-flowing, light read and see what resonates with you. It will leave behind what it needs to and whatever will serve you.

Let the Magic Stay

Just out of my teens, I enrolled for a magic workshop!

Why? Just out of curiosity and time on hand. I had graduated from my 12th year and had time before I had any other compelling engagements. So, the inquisitive part that resides within me came across this advertisement and decided to enrol.

It was a fascinating 4-day workshop, taking us through hand tricks and simple sleight of hand to use in house parties and the likes. But as fascinated as I was, this workshop left me exhausted, disappointed and – if I were to use a stronger word – perhaps, disillusioned!

Suddenly, it felt like there wasn't really any magic anymore. The shows I had seen in the past which looked so fascinating were not anymore as I knew how they were manipulating me all through the years. The audience being fooled, if I might use the word. The magic from the magic entertainment shows was gone for me. I knew how this was done. And I knew now that if I ever attended any magic performance again, leave alone being enthralled, I would probably just relive my disillusionment repeatedly. Needless to say, I never attended a magic show after that. Magic is beautiful, fun and enthralling when you don't know how it's done!

It was like my first realization at two that there might not be a Santa Claus [whilst I still tried to negotiate this with myself saying, maybe I was overreacting] and then, realizing at five that there truly wasn't! You know how that feels? We all know how that feels when we suddenly "grow up" to realise that there are no Santas or magical destinations of the fairy tales!

Why does this have anything to do with what we are talking about?

Where are you doing this in your life? Where are you going, signing up for that information and collecting and hoarding all the data you don't even need or require? Where do you pierce your own magic by knowing too much? Information that doesn't really impact or serve you. Unless you intend to be the magician, of course!

There are places in life we need to know more, and research more. But there are truly places in life where we can simply stay in a place of ignorance and bliss. Things that don't impact us. We don't need to really know anything about other than our own field of influence.

Less is more! Laser-focused knowledge building has its own advantage. Do you know that Uncle Bob or Aunt Samantha who know everything about everything? You most often remember them scoring points over how much they know in every discussion, even in plain conversations. Sometimes, they speak with authority on subjects clearly outside their expertise, making you wonder why they even bother to spend so much time gathering information about that topic. Could they rather put their time and energy to better use and laser-focused growth? Could there be any use? Does it serve them in any way other than scoring some brownie points in closed group conversations and party gossip?

Being multi-faceted and being a data collector are two different things!

This is the problem overthinkers face too. Have you seen people who can't overlook even the most unimportant things on planet earth? It's because they attach a reason and hidden meaning to everything. This is the category of people who think and contemplate so much that they rarely get down to doing. They have great ideas, and sometimes, wonderful strategies because they put so much of thought and analysis into everything they come across, but their attention span on execution is so low [almost non-existent] that they almost always need someone else to implement it.

They spend so much time analyzing things that will never matter to their lives and certainly never serve them that they waste their sharp intellect on only eschewing what has been and what might have been. [The overthinkers are usually sharp and have a higher-than-average IQ].

Accumulating information and overthinking are two different ways to get to the same destination. You can be left so exhausted and disappointed that you could land up wasting all your energy on what doesn't even matter.

Train your brain to focus, hyper-focus even, on things that matter – things that serve you or someone else. When you tend to meander, ask yourself the questions:

- *Does this serve me?*
- *Is it going to further my growth professionally or personally?*

Breaking the Norms

Forgiveness is the new buzzword when it comes to coaches and trainers and everyone who is working with people and their minds. Truth be told, forgiveness can serve you; but so can anger. So can hurt or any other emotion. The key is to find out what the emotion triggers in you. And you will have all categories in your life.

People you want to forgive and can't, people you don't want to forgive at all, people you want to be wary of, people you want to hurt in return. Nothing here is right or wrong. Every emotion, positive and negative, will come and it is absolutely alright.

I am not much of a sucker for forgiveness. I have a few people in my life who motivate me more than anything. And I haven't forgiven them. The anger and the memories keep me motivated whenever I am down and out and about to give up.

I know equally well that the same anger can be unproductive and useless in the case of others I am angry at. Because in those places, I can't channelize it to my advantage. It becomes an energy drainer and it pulls away my focus from more important things. So, that is the area I work on – repeated acceptance and forgiving.

Likewise, a common modern-day fad is to be positive all the time. The positivity pill is all over the place, served in products, services, meditations, books and across social media to a point where in some contexts it is becoming 'Toxic Positivity.'

Going down to your deepest lows can sometimes be the best way to hit back with a bounce to the top. At work, in business, in relationships, in health and most importantly, in self-love too.

So, if there is a time you are down and out, process that low and live it through. You don't always have to fake it till you make it. [*Face it till you Make it* might be a better bet!] Positivity and optimism can also be a habit with time. Sometimes, people who have it easy tend to take optimism so seriously that downfalls and failures are unfathomable for them. They don't know what to do or how to handle these situations.

And that's when the positivity pills floating all around are picked up. Take the pill; it's a great one to have. But use it like you would use a sleeping pill – just enough to induce peace and calm and sleep well.

The "this is My Place" Complex

As I was driving after an exhausting day at work, I decided to stop by at a park close to home. That's something I do often. Sometimes to walk, sometimes to sit on a bench along the boundary lined with flowers, and sometimes just to listen to some instrumental music as it plays. It is refreshing. The entire street is open for parking and as I got near on that day, I saw a car in the middle and occupying two parking spaces! How do people do that?

If there are cars parked one behind the other and you find a place that can accommodate two cars, why would you park in the middle of the two available parking spaces?

You are either a bad driver [but then, you would most likely have an L signage on the car, which is mandatory and you would also most likely not be driving a luxury car!] or you simply don't care.

The world exists because of the many of us who care for the environment, who care for integrity and for those who share space with us [even if we don't know them!]. Also, for those who may be in our place once it's time for us to leave.

This can be throwing the chips packet in the bin even when we were not the ones to eat it. Keeping the toilet seat dry for the next person, putting the chair in place when we get up to leave, holding the door open for the person behind us, holding the elevator button down to keep the doors open till everyone has walked in, returning a borrowed car with the tank full, asking the passenger behind us if it's ok for us to recline our seat, saying a quick prayer when you hear an ambulance siren, using a parking spot responsibly by not taking up the place of a second car, and in every other way. Call it attraction, manifestation or Karma. But what we put out into the world most certainly determines what we receive from it.

When we take responsibility for what we do and how we behave, we will be rewarded with the same too. The category that doesn't, are mostly hoarders. The tendency to grab everything as if there won't be enough is a deep sense of insecurity in some. These are the guys who will go run to get a chair where the guests are more than the chairs, take that extra piece of meat in the gravy when the guests outnumber the pieces, the people who almost always are worried about how things could fall short and show off about how clever they are to have got it first! They are so focused that everything is about them.

Whatever may happen in the world, they always remain at the centre of the universe.

Are you one of them? Do you have a tendency to do this?

Many of us do, and it's not such a bad thing. But recognizing and rectifying it can be liberating. It can give a sense of security that nobody can then take away. And there are lessons to learn from it. We live in a world where there is enough for everyone.

When you are in a space of comfort and security, you attract more of it. In money, in love, in relationships and in health. Life tends to get better and smoother.

Remember ~ ***You are the magic and you only need to get started!***

What's Your Superpower?

There is a wonderful thing about working with founders in their journey. The same kind of joy teachers get when they work closely with their students. It is both an opportunity to revisit our own initial years of the falling and picking it all back again and also a wonderful lesson each day for how their world functions today.

And then, they are all kinds, the nervous ones who will always ask me every time they have to make a decision and the "clever" ones who will ask everything but go do exactly what suits their whim at the last deciding moment. The stalwart business owner, who really kind of knows it all and will not want to be coached. So, they put their 'juniors' into the program, hoping to get something valuable through them, and the novices, who have money in hand from an early retirement they took and know what it is to ride high on the corporate wave, but know little about business and entrepreneurship. Each person, each founder, each decision maker and each business is a unique project that develops into something renewed and refreshed in the end.

If there is one thing I have learnt, both in my journey as a serial entrepreneur and as a Financial Freedom Coach, it is that every person who ever walked this earth has a superpower – something unique and special they bring to the table. Life has a way of making us forget that. About ourselves, about our partners, about our parents, about our siblings and about our friends. The magic in each of us holds the power to proliferate into something that can transform lives and change the world.

When I say this, let's understand that the world changes with every small act of love, kindness and generosity as well as with acts of courage, power and strength. The world needs both constantly to flourish.

Finding our unique superpower is much like our thumbprint or signature. What we have is native to us – a skill that we can hone, that dream we spoke about earlier in this book, a way that we can leave our signature on this world and on the lives of people who crossed our paths. Most people live their entire lives not identifying this or living it fully. Some others chase a dream that they believe is their calling without ever feeling the fulfilment one is supposed to feel when you are living your magic.

But you know what your superpower is. Dig into your own patterns; what is it that you can do for hours together, lose track of time and never really get tired or exhausted from it?

What is a skill that you think you are really good at and you have been told that by your closest people too? Maybe, you are already honing and using that skill. Maybe, you know but you think it can't be more than a hobby because it is not lucrative. Maybe, you have tried and not excelled at it. So, you have put it away.

My superpower is the ability to learn and functionally master anything new in the fastest Turn Around Time [TAT]. When I say fastest, I compare it to anyone else who has a similar educational background and knowledge about the subject as me, meaning where our 'Zeroes' are the same. I am a Finance professional. I pursued MBA after I got done with my CA. I concurrently pursued an MA in English Literature because I am a language enthusiast.

During my school years, I spent time on different musical instruments, getting formally trained in one string instrument [sitar] and all the others being just 'trying my hand' or 'playing by the ear.' This included the guitar, keyboards, percussion and violin.

I pursued photography, doing a small course from an institute and then, spending endless hours with my camera and film rolls to get a hang of experimenting with different kinds of genres. At that time, there were no digital cameras and photography was about the rolls that needed to be developed and then, pictures printed out before we knew what the result of an entire shoot was going to be. I also did a short stint in the form of a series of photo shoots, initially for some friends, and then, for some upcoming models who wanted to have a good and reasonably priced portfolio!

The passing of my mother followed closely by the Covid 19 pandemic and a series of lockdowns were a string of events that were deeply disturbing and difficult. It started with my mom's sudden passing in December 2019 and within three months, we were in lockdown due to Covid 19. Those were the most gruelling 12 months with on and off eases on the lockdown, but mostly house confinement.

Some people in our lives hold our life together. And when that bubble suddenly vanishes, it is like grappling in the dark for really long. As anyone who has read any part of this book or has engaged with me in person or on social, it is a known fact that these have been the most difficult months of my life. For someone like me who has been so much in the happy space, no matter what was happening around me, this was a truly difficult task at this time.

In quick succession, I also had another loss during covid that was deeply upsetting. I leave that for another time to talk about. Both these put together, I had hit an all-time low. Learning came to my rescue. In the lockdowns, I devoured learning through online platforms like never before. Keyboards, Spanish, Music reading, advanced PowerPoint, advanced Excel, Django [coding]. It won't be wrong to say that learning and my time spent on upskilling actually kept me sane and busy during this difficult phase.

So, our superpower is not only something which can be made lucrative, make us money, and bring us fame or success, it is most likely also something that can drown us and through that drowning, save us in difficult times. What is your superpower? What is something you enjoy doing, which inspires and soothes you?

Opportunity and Being Ready for It

How prepared are you if the opportunity knocks on your door now? No really. Think about it.

The fortune game has a lot to do with what you are doing every day and hour, to prepare yourself for the day when opportunity knocks. But still, most people wait to do things that do not really contribute to that preparation in any way. And so, when an opportunity arrives, you feel not ready enough, or not fit enough or not good enough to grab it.

There is no person on this planet who hasn't got at least five great, larger-than-life opportunities in their lives! No one! Yet, there is less than 5% of the world population who has grabbed it and made the most of it.

Why? What was different about them? Were they more talented or better skilled or had a higher IQ or simply got lucky?

They were better prepared!

Don't Miss the Point

One of the strongest emotions people can feel, is regret.

What would you regret if you were to die tomorrow? What would you wish you had a little more time to do?

This question is enough to bring up a series of answers that flutter through your mind right now. I can see that!

Maybe, you regret not having completed your education. Maybe, you regret not having expressed your love to someone. Maybe, you regret having settled for a marriage or a career or a home that was not your choice. Maybe, you regret losing time or not doing enough to preserve your health. Maybe, you regret not having worked on yourself more. Maybe, you regret letting someone go.

We all have something we wish we had done differently. That we successfully wrap up and tuck away. I hope the first half of the book where we worked with our past memories and stories has helped you open up and process whatever you needed to and that you have come this far clearer and cleaner.

And yet, since we are always 'work in progress' as humans, ask yourself, if you die tomorrow, what are the three regrets you would have?

Of these, can you undo or redo any today?

Recently, I read an anecdote which seemed very powerful to me. A Chemical Engineer who had invented dynamite and several other explosives in the 19th century was both powerful and wealthy.

One day, he opened the morning paper to find an obituary written for him. It was an error and he had no idea how it had happened. The obituary mentioned how he was the inventor of dynamite and other explosives, and it announced his death. There seemed to be a goof up on that, and in a rage, he reached out to the newspaper office. The newspapers were printed and already circulated, there was little that could be done to undo what had occurred.

But what was waiting to happen was far more intense for him. Comments and reactions to the news of his death started falling on his ears. He heard about what people felt and how very few were really even mourning him. Follow-up snippets and articles spoke about how many were criticizing him for his inventions which had caused the deaths of thousands of people and would continue to do so in the years to come. His obituary and legacy seemed to be so negative that they filled him with regret. This is surely not how he wanted people to remember him when he really died.

He realized that all his wealth and success would bring him nothing more than the ill-will and anger of people once he was gone because he had no legacy to leave behind.

This man went on to then institute a Global level Foundation to honour good work and award those who excelled in the fields of Science, Mathematics, Politics and even Peace. With his realisation, he built a legacy of his choice so that people would remember him after he was gone for centuries together. He literally rewrote his obituary.

He died in 1896. The world knows the prizes he instituted as the Nobel Prize. He was Alfred Nobel.

What would you like your obituary to read? What would you like for people's reaction to be when you are gone?

Write down your own obituary. And then, see what you need to include in your road map to go from where you are to where you want to be!

What's the Price of Your Dream?

Opportunity cost is a very important part of tallying one's ROI and understanding what the real adjusted profit might be when you strike a deal! In simplified terms, for everything you are saying YES to, you are saying NO to something else.

Read that again!

Whenever you give your time, energy or money to one thing, you are keeping it from something else. Opportunity cost is the value of the opportunity "lost."

And every decision we make in our professional and personal lives always has a price to pay for it. Sometimes, this runs deeper than just a monetary value.

On a Sunday morning, if a college friend gets in touch to ask you if you can meet them for a round of golf and you have already promised your 4-year-old to take them out on a day picnic. Whichever way you decide has an opportunity cost to it.

The same amplifies and applies to every decision you make. What you do will always keep you from something else you might have done!

If you function from a space of evaluating the price you are paying, you most likely will know where you want to stop.

This book is about money. About the mindset work you can do and some practical guidelines to get clearer about your goals and road maps. But while you do all of this, it's important you don't exclude the people that matter. Do what is important to you. Know what are the biggest wins you want from your life. And with every financial goal you set, do set it in the context of your life goals. One of the reasons we talk about purpose and our *Ikigai* before we talk about goal setting in this book is because the purpose is a much larger thing. It engulfs and touches every part of our lives and is not limited to money or success.

If you have everything in the world, all the money you aspire for and success, but don't have love and companionship, nobody understands you and you don't have friends to vent out with, and your health is not the way you would like it to be, and you are forced to spend your evenings alone each day, would you be happy?

Define what success means to you. Define how much is really enough for you to find the balanced life of your dreams. Determine who and what is important to you and make that a part of your journey.

One of the first skills in money management is to account for every price in whatever form that you pay in order to make a profit!

Is Bigger Better?

If I were to ask you how much money you want to make in your life so that you feel you are financially free, what is your likely answer?

Do you know how many millions make a billion? Or a trillion? Do you have a reference point for that?

Let's give it a point of reference that Tony Robbins has used in one of his works. Do you know how many days a million seconds translate into? Surely, you hadn't thought of this one before! According to Robbins [and I calculated after reading], a million seconds is roughly 12 days!

What about a billion seconds? How many days would that be? Ok, wait, let's take a wild guess!

32 years! Yes, sounds crazy right?

A million seconds and a billion seconds is 12 days and 32 years! A trillion? 32,000 years.

Do you get the perspective Now?

Why is this calculation relevant? Because when we throw out a figure to the question I asked at the beginning, most of us would answer in figures too small or outrageously big or whatever. But most of the time, the figure is neither calculated nor planned nor do we have a point of reference. They are ad-hoc figures thrown into our vocabulary and then into our minds.

So, if your answer is I want to be a millionaire or a billionaire, how clear are these terms to you? How much do you need, want and aspire for? Can we have different kinds and levels of goals to get there in a stepped-up manner rather than a single leap?

You know [spiritually, of course] that most of the money you make in your lifetime is not going to be enjoyed by you but by others. Most of the planning and goal setting and becoming-a-millionaire stories are for what you are going to leave behind for others.

What is it that you really need to live your best life with absolute financial freedom? Not a billion, methinks.

After a point, the numbers start blurring and so do those goals. If your goal is to be a billionaire, and right now, you make $20,000 a year, then the billionaire goal stops looking real to you. And so, the smaller steps you can take today to get there are never taken. And before you know it, 10, 20, 50 years can pass. Just like that.

Do you think it could be easier to set a goal for your income to move up to $100,000? Five times what you are at. A big jump, but possible, visible and clearly achievable. Do you also think that when you get to $100,000 and get down to a new goal setting exercise, $500,000 would look achievable to you? Of course, it would!

Chunking down your goals will make all the difference. Know fully well that each milestone counts and get there before you begin the journey to the next. And along the way, how much you really want can also get clearer. If "billions" is simply a place you desire to reach where you will have complete financial freedom and you have never quite worked out the numbers. Then, probably, what you really aspire for could be less. Or more.

Bigger isn't always better. Sometimes, knowing what the big thing means to you, and what you define for yourself is what matters.

Your aspiration might be to give your kids education, have an easy-flowing retirement fund, travel the world and live stress-free in the countryside.

Or you may want to work till your last living day, travel the world and set up new businesses, provide for your family and live life king-size with holiday homes and a luxury yacht.

You could be the one who wants a beach-front home and a second home on an island, live life on your terms and run a charity that would be your legacy.

It doesn't matter which of these (or something else maybe) you are. We will find a plan in the subsequent chapter for you!

Ignore the Naysayers

There is an ancient tale that I heard on the first course that I did of the Art of Living many moons ago. As you already know, I went on to follow the practice through different levels, and eventually, also took up the training to become a faculty, as I mentioned earlier.

Inspiring stories told in a simple format are often thrown in by teachers on this course to illustrate certain points.

One such is the story of the donkey being led from one place to another by a father-son duo.

As they both walk alongside the donkey, a passerby says to them, "How silly are both of you! The donkey who is used to carrying weight is walking free. Why isn't one of you sitting on the donkey?"

The father-son look at each other, albeit a bit embarrassed and figure it is silly indeed. The father makes the boy sit on the donkey and they restart their journey.

A little ahead another passerby says, this time to the boy, "You are riding the donkey while your elder is walking beside you. Where are your manners?"

The father doesn't think much of it but the boy is scared of being judged. He jumps off the donkey and convinces his father to get onto it.

Move a little further and another says, "You are making your little boy walk while you are comfortably seated on the donkey. A mother would never do that!" [And, boy, we know that can hurt a father more than anything; being told a mother would never do what he is doing.]

With mixed feelings about all the judgements, the father picks up the boy and gets him to sit on the donkey too. So now both of them are riding the donkey. The donkey is a small and frail creature and both the father and son robust in their build. The donkey is unable to take the weight. It falls and injures itself. And the trip they had set out to do comes to an unexpected and unfortunate end.

Moral of the Story in our Context – Everyone will have opinions. We do too. And most of the time, we share our opinions easily, without much thought or processing. Something that might stay with the listener long after it was said might only be a passing comment made by the speaker. The mind is a fragile object, and you will always be inclined to hold on to any criticism far more than a compliment.

Steer away from the Naysayers. From the ones who sit by the curb and pass comments or hoot when you perform. If they could do better than what you are doing, they would be doing it. *Read that Again!*

What Are You Avoiding?

Here's another story. Two monks were travelling together to a different village where their master had asked them to go visit. The route was a rural one with streams along the way and a beautiful pebble-strewn path.

As they walked along the way, one of them saw a woman walk up to them. She was stark naked.

Monk A was flustered and looked the other way. After all, he wasn't supposed to see such things and it would be a sin if he continued looking her way.

Monk B continued to walk his path, not at all perturbed with who was coming towards him. As the woman neared, she asked the monks to help her to cross the stream. Monk B placed a shawl that he had on his shoulder over her and carried her to drop her to the other side. She thanked him and left once she had crossed over. He crossed the stream back onto this side and continued walking.

The rest of the way, both of them remained silent. It was a heavy silence.

When they reached the monastery almost 3 hours later, Monk A said to Monk B, "I am going to tell the Master that you halted and spoke to a naked woman. That you carried a naked woman. How could you do that?"

Monk B replied, "I carried her for 60 seconds; you have been carrying her for the last 3 hours!"

A simple rule of life! If you are avoiding something with all your might, you are probably focusing more on it than you realize! It may be entering your thoughts and your subconscious and maybe, you manifest that repeatedly. This is not only mind-work, it is also a fact that can be proved through science.

What is it that you are trying hard to avoid in your life right now? How is it repeatedly showing up?

Can you let it go?

Confidence Comes From Having a Plan B

A third!

A king visited a revered saint in a small town in Southern India. After a day's visit and meditations and spending time in the natural precincts of the Ashram, the king made a donation to the saint to contribute to all the good work he was doing.

Upon this, the saint called for a box through one of his disciples and handed it over to the king. He told the king to keep this box and hold it as valuable. And to open it only when he was really, really in trouble or in a difficulty he couldn't handle and he would find an answer. The condition was that he could open it only once. After which, the box would have no value anymore.

The king left with gratitude in his heart.

On an occasion, the king was threatened by war on all sides and his army was caving in because they were thoroughly outnumbered. He was tempted to open the box, but then, he thought to himself, '*I can open it only once, maybe next time. What if something bigger happens?*'

He found a way out of the war and won it. All along, the box gave him confidence that if he were to need it, he had something to help him out. His Plan B.

Another time, his entire kingdom saw famine and the rains were delayed further. He discussed with his queen about this. What could be worse when as a king, he was finding it difficult to protect his people? But he decided he would find a different way. Armed with the knowledge that he had the box for help if he needed it, he struck a deal with his neighbouring kingdoms and found a way to protect his people and keep them provided for until it rained that year. His subjects were thrilled to see how able a king they had that he could even find solutions for natural calamities.

For years together, problems came up and the king used his effort, intellect and his team of wise people to find ways out of every situation. The fact that he had a secret tool to manage anything if it ever became unmanageable, gave him a sense of comfort.

Many years later, when the king was a bit older and the prince had now grown into a young man, the prince led the army to a small battle and came back injured. The best doctors and medical practitioners were brought in but the prince's health didn't seem to improve. The prince was the next king. He was brave, intelligent and kind. Saving the prince was not only the need of a loving father but also the most prudent thing to do for the entire kingdom.

At last, the king decided to open the box and use the tool this time. After all, what could be more difficult than this time when the future of the entire kingdom hinged on the recovery of the prince?

The king brought out the box he had safely kept treasured for so many years. And he opened it carefully, knowing fully well that he was going to find the answer.

Inside was a note which read, "This too shall pass."

Jackal and the Lion [Which Side Are You on]

And my favourite one!

A lazy man who prayed to God every day often wondered why his life wasn't getting any better. All his atheist friends were flourishing and doing well. They had beautiful homes and loving spouses and their kids were doing well at school and they were in great jobs earning enough to enjoy the good life.

One day, when he got back from a reunion with his friends, he was angry with God.

'*Everyone but I seem to be doing well,*' he thought to himself. So, he had a tiff with God. Angry as he was, he threatened God that he would stop praying altogether if nothing was done immediately about the state his life was in.

That night in his dreams, he saw a jackal sitting on the side of a road and a mighty lion throwing leftovers for him. He woke up startled and wondered what the dream meant. He realized it would be an answer from God. So, he thought to himself, '*God is listening to me. He has provided for me. I am going to meet someone who is going to provide for me soon.*'

Days passed and weeks too. Nothing changed. He was beginning to get agitated again. Every time he would complain to God, he would see the same dream at night. But nobody appeared in real to help him out or provide for him.

That night, he gave God an ultimatum. "If nothing moves in two days," he said, "I will truly stop praying."

That night, God appeared in his dreams.

He asked with the eagerness and the wide-eyed awe of a child, "You show me the dream and give me hope each time I ask you. But nothing has changed and no one has come to help me out. Why are you doing this?"

God answered "Oh, fool! I have made you the Lion!"

Who is Watching?

If you have interacted with me, you know that I am clear with my boundaries especially when it comes to my ethics and ideologies. It's also one of the reasons I never joined my dad in business. We all have ideologies that resonate with us, but when they don't align within teams, teams can disintegrate very fast.

It was past 1 A.M. Mumbai streets are never really empty. And often, especially on weekends, the traffic signal system which is usually put off at 12 midnight, remains functional longer. Weekends are a time people are in a holiday head space and tend to speed up more. Incidents of drunken driving also are much higher. This is the likely reason why during Friday and Saturday nights most traffic signals are still functional even way past midnight.

As we approached a traffic light that was red, I brought the car to halt. There were no cars in front of me and none behind me yet. Our light was red. And it's a four-road junction. My dad who was sitting in the backseat was getting restless. I could see from the rearview mirror that he wanted to say something but was unsure. You know that moment when you almost open your mouth and then change your mind?

Finally, he said, "It's 1 A.M and the traffic light is on by mistake obviously. What are we waiting for?"

I said, "For our light to turn green. There is a logic why the traffic light is on at this hour, I am sure."

He asked, "There is no car anywhere. I don't see the point in waiting. Who is watching anyway?"

"I am," I replied.

Conscience is the small voice inside us which tells us what to do even when nobody else is watching! No, I didn't say this aloud, my dad doesn't buy into these things easily anyway. His theories are very different from mine. So, no point. But since I was the one driving that night, it had to be my point of view that prevailed.

What we do, the ethics we decide to set for ourselves, and the standards and ideologies we build are not for someone else. They are for us. It is not about who will get to know or who will watch; it is about what you intend to do and how truly you will stick to it.

There are people who call themselves "honest" and they are – until it is convenient! To each his own, and how much you want to flex your ideology is always your call. But define what it is for you and then work within the paradigm. Sometimes, in the bid to get quick success, you might be tempted by people or by situations to take the shortcut! The short cuts can often be the wrong cuts too. Step back and evaluate. Measure it against the ideology you have set up for yourself. Then, take the call.

Don't Be Bunny!

Have you watched Ranbir Kapoor starrer "*Yeh Jawaani Hai Deewani*?" Bunny, the character played by Ranbir, is prancing all over the place, wanting to always be where the action is.

He is a vagabond-ish traveller and photographer, always on the run to try and catch the next best thing. Best described, he is in a constant state of FOMO [for the unversed *Fear of Missing Out*].

At one point, the character Naina, portrayed by Deepika Padukone says to him, "*Life mein kitna bhi try karo, kuch na kuch toh Chhootega hi..*" ("However much you try in life, something or the other will be left undone")

When I saw this movie for the first time, this dialogue brought a point straight home. Truly no matter what we do and how much we run and try and push everything into our time, we will always miss out on something. A profound way of explaining the opportunity cost concept so beautifully?

Also, a simple life lesson. Be present. Be where you are, fully. Enjoy this moment, this day, this situation fully.

When at work, work. When on a holiday, enjoy. When with someone you love, be with them fully.

Multitasking in recent years has become a skill everyone wants to master. But when multitasking, it is even more important to be able to do that task in hand with complete presence, before moving on to the next. Multitasking is, at best, like juggling. When you juggle multiple things, your sense of being and doing 100% has to be stronger and sharper!

The next time you find yourself tempted to open your social media account to check or text someone, when you are out for dinner with a friend, don't be Bunny!

When you are watching a movie with your partner and your work phone rings, [and it's after work hours] don't be Bunny!

When you are working on a project, chasing a deadline and are tempted because your buddy asked you for an evening out for drinks, don't be Bunny!

When you look back, your strongest memories come from the moments you were 100% in what you were doing. Being present can make the most mundane tasks enjoyable and memorable.

Just don't be Bunny!

Where are you keeping yourself small because you don't think you have enough skills, or talent, or something someone else has?

Where are you keeping success away by avoiding failure?

Where are you getting influenced by what everyone is telling you rather than what you believe from within?

What is your view of the "this is my place" complex?

Where are you collecting too much information and never putting it to use?

What price are you willing to pay for your dream?

What norms are you willing to break?

Most importantly, what superpower are you keeping from the world?

Where are you being Bunny?

Chapter 3.5

Your Personalized Money Management System I {Determining Your Financial Freedom Threshold}

Surveys and research across the internet show interesting figures on how inflation has been impacting the lives of people. One survey suggests that 56% of people who earn enough money to provide for all their needs year-on-year, might be broke by the time they are 65 years old. Another says, that of all the Lottery Winners, 95% will lose their entire win in 3 years. It's a documented fact that more than 95% of individuals are not eligible for pension after retirement.

General Insurance Companies do not cover individuals above the age of 70 for Medical Insurance. Term Insurance doesn't cover life after the insured attains the age of 75 in most cases. The Fixed Term Deposits are at an all-time low interest rate of less than 6% per annum, with no benefits or subsidies given to senior citizens.

In short, there is little or no financial stability that is inbuilt into our system. It is almost prohibitive to grow old. If you are reading this book, money management and financial freedom matter to you. What age you are at, what gender or where you live doesn't change the above facts much. You are already in a bracket where you may be facing some of these challenges, or you are going to get there someday.

What can be scary is that as time passes by, the disparity between the rich and the poor is getting increasingly wider. All the above points have a combined effect on what your money position might be when you are 60 years old.

Improved healthcare and enhanced lifestyles have significantly increased longevity, which means people have more years on hand and resultantly higher total costs after retirement. Inflation and reducing or no income can tweak the situation further against you.

In one of the earlier chapters, we talked about fear and overthinking. On the other end of the spectrum is complete ignorance, or denial might be a better word.

Many of us are on this spiral, running our daily lives, ticking off tasks, running errands and living pay cheque to pay cheque. Our wins come from buying a home or a better car each time or better holidays than our neighbours and friends.

But this book is not written to scare you; it is written with an intention to inspire you and give you tangible systems that you can work with. To understand the paradigms of Money Generation, and more importantly, money management which can ensure a lifetime of comfortable and luxurious living with what you define to be a happy life.

Let's start with understanding how you can make money work for you. What paradigms determine this math and how you can work on turning these in your favour?

3 Paradigms to Make Money Work for You

1. **Time**

   Time plays a very important role in the way we generate and manage money. The earlier you get financial education and start taking charge of your money, the more chances there will be of growing and multiplying it exponentially in your lifetime. The compounding effect comes from the factor of time. Starting early is key, but that doesn't mean you have to regret not having started yet.

   Wherever you are, start now. And let time work in your favour.

   Example: Let's take the example of Warren Buffet. Buffet started investing at the age of 13. If we look at the wealth he has created in his life and run a simple math, it is clear that the number of years he has invested and the sheer year-on-year growth factor are what have helped him compound the amounts. And still, Buffet has been open in saying that he thinks he started too late!

2. **Rate of Return**

   Traditional systems such as term deposits and conventional holdings in jewellery have today become low-paying assets. They don't really produce any returns that can count. The safety or security element they bring is much higher as compared to many asset groups, but if you want to be in the game for growth, it is important for you to understand what category of assets can give you the highest returns with the least risk fix.

How much should the ROI per annum be if you want to retire 20 years from now? Or in 10? 5?

Obviously, there comes the third. How much do you have to invest and stay invested?

3. **Disposable Capital**

The initial amount you might have available with you to invest is the most simplified definition of the word "capital." It can mean many different things in more advanced concepts, but we restrict our usage to this meaning in the book.

Investments most often happen out of savings. Savings happen most often out of income. There are exceptions to this rule like to every other rule. You may have inherited or received amounts from someone. You might decide to exit from an existing asset to raise an amount for investment. You might be a smart saver and always manage to put aside an amount to invest. You might be a smart planner and use the rolling concept to your benefit, increasing the investment amount slightly at each exit and re-entry.

If you learn this one skill well, it will always leave more disposable capital in your hand which you can use to invest. An important part of the Return-on-Investment Formula, it is only a mathematical logic that

Increased Disposable Capital = Increased Investment Possibility

Four Things You Can Do to Increase Your Disposable Capital:

1. ***Improve your Capacity to Generate Income** – Upskilling, starting a side hustle, increasing your productivity, and delegating to better and larger teams are just some ways to be able to generate more income, which naturally, can put more money into your hands to start with.*
2. ***Restructuring your Assets and Income** – Sometimes the assets you hold or a business or occupation you are holding on to are not the best options available to you. You might be aware, but emotions get in the way. Selling an asset which is close to your heart or has a sentimental value can be difficult. But it can be a prudent thing to do. If you have assets that add to your balance sheet [second home, weekend home, vehicles, properties you don't use or earn from] but do not add to your liquidity, it might be time for you to run a thorough audit of all you have and how these could be optimally utilised to bring liquidity into your life.*
3. ***Steer Away from Instant Gratification** – The influx of the internet and increasing social media*

growth has us engulfed from all sides. This means stronger messaging, more advertising and more opportunity to purchase immediately. As opposed to how things were sold and bought earlier, the world around us is currently pushing things literally in our face. How often does it happen that after you buy something on an impulse or to avail of a discount you realize you don't like it as much? You might not even use it or sometimes might give it away. It's a good idea to set parameters for your buys, especially if you have a tendency to be an impulsive shopper. Online shopping is more accessible and the temptation may be more. You can set your cards and digital payment systems to have a limit. Or even disable some. Make the buy difficult. Delaying a buy will make the impulsive or temptation buying urge go away.

4. ***Gift yourself a Mentor/Advisor*** – *Ever wondered why all top-performing athletes hire and then stick to the best coaches in the world? Every successful athlete, sportsperson, musician, actor, and billionaire will tell you how the right coaching and mentoring worked for them at different stages of their lives to get to where they are.*

   A third-person view, a bounce pad approach and being able to constantly keep you on track is the job of a coach.

   Investment advice can also come from a financial expert or a broking firm. The best way is to identify areas of your life you want to upskill and get sound advice for them. And then, try and find a Mentor or Coach who can be instrumental in working with you in that area.

At the outset, this might sound like an added expense, but as I have said elsewhere in the book, root for the input-output ratio. If investing this amount brings you an exponential multiplier, then it's one of the best investments you can make! What could the metabolism of this decision be?

You now know the 3 paradigms of making money work for you. But how do you really use these? How do you even know what amount you would require to feel financially free?

Let's start from the beginning!

The Money Management System

To set up your personalized Money Management System, the first thing to look at is, how much money do you really need to have in order to live a happy and financially free life. This can mean different things to different people and there is no plug-and-play formula.

So, get a pen and paper and we will build the system together with guidelines, calculations and inputs from the upcoming pages in this chapter.

This is interesting work and can be a bit exhausting too. But let's make it fun! Maybe, you can whip up a hot coffee or make yourself a drink of your choice and sit down with your phone and laptop. You may want to look up your statements or check your bank messages or dig into some files on either. When you are ready, let's begin!

Let's start with defining what we can call your **Happiness Fund**. This is the disposable capital you require as a lump sum, which you can use to invest so that the returns on these investments can take care of all your financial outflows. This also means, that *when you have your Happiness Fund ready and begin to invest it smartly, you can maintain your level of financial goals without having to work again in your life!*

Logically then, what we need first is to calculate your unique Happiness Fund Value.

Your Financial Freedom Plan

We can do this in three parts:

1. ***Level 1 – Financial Security***

   Financial Security needs are at the bottom, most akin to the lowest grid of Maslow's Theory of Needs. Food, clothing and shelter. And in current times, it must be adapted to also include insurance and a small amount kept aside for contingencies.

   But really, what does security mean to you? Based on where we live, how we were raised, how big or small our family is, the vocation or profession we are in, many things determine what security means to different people.

   In the format given below, the financial security section contains all the expenses that are needed to cover your basic living costs.

This slab contains housing costs [Mortgage Payments or Rent as applicable], Utility Payments [Electricity, Phone, Water Bills, Property Tax, etc.,] Food/Groceries, Transportation Costs [EMI for Car, Public Transport, Fuel Costs, etc.]

This amount should be the actuals that you incur/require for each of these headings per month. Then, annualize it by multiplying the sum total by 12.

In this slab, we also add insurance [Life & Medical Insurance]. *Add in the premiums that you pay for life and medical insurance.*

The total amount reached in this level assures you of financial security, which covers the basic living costs and a little safety by contributing to insurance.

Add in a Medical Fund for all things insurance won't cover, more like a contingency cost.

However, you might want to include something else which is a basic need or brings you security. To make this list your own, add everything that you define as 'security' and 'necessities.'

2. ***Level 2 – Financial Independence***

Financial Independence is over and above the security level. Things that make you feel good, that give you and your loved ones, comfort. This again is personal and can be different for different people. So, it's important for you to list out what you would like to have and include it in your monthly expenses to have a comfortable life.

Make this list and jot down everything you want to put. Next to each item, put the estimated spend you need to budget for each of these. Once you have arrived at the figure of your Financial Security Level, we get to that little extra that you, of course, want to have!

In this slab, you add in the costs of clothes and accessories that you would buy in the year [estimated]. Throw in the dine-outs and entertainment bills that you would want to provide for.

Maybe, we can add things like some *upskilling, gym memberships and travel once in a while.* This is a personal choice and remember to add in what matters to you to improve the quality of your life and feel like you are not on a budget anymore!

3. ***Level 3 – Financial Freedom***

Financial freedom is the level where you stretch and go beyond just needs and comforts, into luxury, your dreams and your fantasies. This can be in the form of assets you wish to own, trips you want to take, or a charity you want to start. Anything that you might think is a bit lavish right now!

This is the component to move from independence to complete freedom. It is the time to live up your dreams in this slab. What is it you want to do once you are in this slab?

It could be a foundation or charity you want to set up, a luxury yacht you want to get, or that weekend home by the river you are dreaming about.

*In the Financial Models, remember if you have the capital at this point and invest in the asset of your dreams with a complete payment, you still add up your opportunity cost in this slab. Which means, you buy an asset for Rs. 50,00,000 with your own money which you have by then. But the basic fixed interest on this amount if you made a secure investment is 6%. So, your opportunity cost per year is 50,00,000 * 6/100 = 3,00,000.*

Let's take an example and work these three levels out for a better understanding of the formula.

	Example	**Your Figures**
1. Housing Costs {Mortgage, Rental Payments or Opportunity Cost if Purchased with Owned Funds}	50,000	
2. Utility Bills {Electricity, Property Tax, Water, Phones, Internet, etc.}	5,000	
3. Food and Groceries	20,000	
4. Transportation {Car, Fuel, Public Transport used, etc.}	10,000	
5. Insurance {Life and Medical}	5,000	
6. Emergency/Medical Fund	10,000	
Total Cost per Month	**1,00,000**	
Financial Security Level [A]	**12,00,000**	

	Example	Your figures
1. Clothes & Accessories	10,000	
2. Dining Out & Entertainment	10,000	
3. Gym Membership/Club/ Other	5,000	
4. Travel	20,000	
5. Upskilling	2,000	
6. Other Costs to Add on in this Slab	5,000	
Total Costs per Month	**52,000**	
Costs per Year	**6,24,000**	
Financial Independence Level [B]	**18,24,000**	
{Financial Security A + Costs for Financial Independence}		

	Example	Your figures
1. Foundation/Charity	25,000	
2. Dream Second Home	35,000	
3. Bigger Car/Luxury Yacht	20,000	
4. Any other Luxury Dream	20,000	
Total Costs per Month	**1,00,000**	
Costs per Year	**12,00,000**	
Financial Freedom [C]	**30,24,000**	
{B + Costs per year for Financial Freedom}		

I have put ad-hoc amounts to illustrate the principle and the process. The second column is for you. Put in the amounts and add rows as you please. Your Financial Freedom Plan could run into pages, and that's fine, great!

Just chunk it down to arrive at three different levels. If you have a fourth level step up in the middle, say you have a lot to add to your Financial Independence Level and your Financial Freedom Level is much above my simplified list. You might want to add a level in the middle and call it, maybe Financial Scalability. Or whatever name you like. Based on the range you want to travel between where you are and where you want to get, you can devise slabs and play around with this sheet.

The first and important one remains Financial Security and the last one must culminate into complete financial freedom.

You now have three levels [or more!] for yourself at which, you achieve three [or more!] different levels of financial goals. Remember that the additions at each stage can be different based on what your needs and desires are. The list is indicative of what you can add in each slab stage. You can and must determine your own Security, Independence and Freedom Levels.

Taking the example forward, you can also determine three different levels of Funds/Capital that you need to have in order to be able to generate these income levels.

Let me explain. Why did we work out the three levels of what you need per year for three goals?

Now, we know how much you need to generate each year, year-on-year, to live your life on any of the three levels, ***without never having to work a day again!*** It also answers the question I asked earlier in this chapter. How much do you think you need to have in order to live your dream life?

This is the answer. If you need to build a Happiness Fund or Capital over time – so that just by investing that fund you can take care of all your Financial Needs – what would that amount have to be?

Happiness Fund Calculations for All Levels

Say [as per the example] you require 12,00,000 per year for your Financial Security Level Goal. At the least, the Return on Investment is 6% {FDs} and it can be more aggressive if we take higher risks on variable returns. Let's take a conservative benchmark.

*To Generate 12,00,000 each year at 6% return, you need a Happiness Fund of 12,00,000 * 100/6 = Rs. 2,00,00,000 [Two Crores].*

Happiness Fund at Financial Security Level = 2 Crores

Applying the same 6% calculation, *the amount you need for Financial Independence is Rs. 18,24,000 per year.*

*18,24,000 * 100/6 = 3,04,00,000 [Three Crores and Four Lacs]*

Happiness Fund at Financial Independence Level = 3.04 Crores

*With the identical calculation for the Financial Freedom Level, we apply 30,24,000 * 100/6 = 5,04,00,000 [Five Crores and Four lacs]*

Happiness Fund at Financial Freedom Level = 5.04 Crores

Similarly, you can calculate your unique Happiness Fund Value for any additional slabs you have built for yourself.

You would, at this stage, have your three financial goals in place. It is going to be exclusive for you, worked out by you. It could be much higher or much lower from our example here. Use the example only as an illustration to find all your parameters.

At this point, before we move into the next chapter, complete all your workings here. All the goals and the Happiness Fund you need to have in order to achieve them over time.

Building in buffers at every level always helps. So, you might want to add buffers when estimating costs and also be conservative when planning returns. You now know that you do not require to reach for everything at once. As you move up to save, earn more, invest wisely and generate returns, you can move up the notch, reaching Financial Security at first and then moving up the other levels.

Finding your Happiness Fund figures for all Levels can do two things right now.

On one hand, you may feel a sense of relief realizing that what you thought was a long-drawn journey into the unknown, looks more tangible and attainable.

On the other hand, you might also be worried because it sounds too much. Sometimes looking the other way feels like an easier thing to do. Not sitting down to ever work out what you really need can be easier than facing it and putting all your calculations to paper.

Trust me, this is a great start to do all these workings and come to the conclusion of what you need to achieve.

Now that you have the 'What,' the 'How' will find its way to you!

Chapter 3.6

Your Personalized Money Management System II {Investment Buckets and Asset Classes Under Each}

In India, there is an ancient saying which goes somewhat like this "You can take a horse to the water but you can't make him drink it!"

What you did so far is about numbers, about looking in the right direction to work out the Happiness Fund that you need in order to reach different Levels of Financial Gains in your life.

As obvious as it sounds, we sometimes don't understand that this is unique for each of us. If you are someone who lives with a family of four in the midst of New York or Tokyo or Mumbai, you most likely have much higher figures to reach for, as compared to if you are a family of two in a city such as Hanoi (Vietnam) or Bangkok (Thailand).

Other than the location and size of the family, your figures can change drastically based on your lifestyle, the vocation you are in, your age bracket and if you already have assets.

The plan is yours and you have to build it from here. I can share some hacks, tips and examples to assist you, but only you know what works for you. And, of course, you will tweak it along the way as well. Some things to think about before we go further:

1. *Is Advantage Real?* Have you seen a running track where athletes are placed in a staggered position? The runner on the innermost track is way behind the runner on the outermost. Every runner knows that this staggering is a way to make the game fair so that every runner runs an equal distance. Is there an advantage then? For the outermost for being ahead? Or for the innermost for having the shortest circle to run?

   No! But can this play on the minds of the runners? Can being ahead or visually having to run the smallest circle give a stronger stand point to the runner in their mind? Perhaps!

   In an ideal scenario, it can take a person about 8 to 20 years to be financially free.

   Remember, although time is an essential component to make money work for you, and for the compounding effect to kick in, that does not mean that you can't win if you are starting late. The advantage is a perceived one.

   The 3 Paradigm Rule is precisely for that. If you don't have one on your side, you can still make the other two [or at least one] work for you!

   Learning to find these 3 paradigms and picking the one that you can use to your advantage is a great starting point for your plan.

2. *Your Risk Appetite.* Now that you have evaluated the time you have, in the context of the Happiness Fund you require to build, you can plan the risk you are willing to take.

   Typically, the safest investment options come at a 5-6% per annum returns. The more aggressive ones, with higher risk involved, can fetch you about 12-18% per annum. This is the window in which you can play when making your plan. Anything more aggressive than 18% are more niche investments and I deliberately keep them out of this book since the risk analysis plays a big role in these. By now, you know that the time you have in your plan and the returns are inversely proportionate. Which means, if you have more time in hand you can be conservative with your investments and opt for a lower rate of interest putting safety first. As the time in hand reduces, you might want to look at getting more aggressive with at least a part of your investments to achieve higher returns.

   Let's say on your way up, the first few years when you start out and your risk appetite can be higher, and you are still earning regularly, you can incline in the favour of a higher rate of interest and take the risk. After a point, when you want to tilt in the favour of safety over high returns, you can start moving investments to the other side. This way, you can take advantage of aggressive returns while you can afford to and balance it out without compromising on the safety factor too much.

3. *Save More in the Future.* Maintain a discipline where hereon, with every incremental revenue [appraisal in a job, increased salary or profit in business that you draw] you will save a component.

   So, if your incremental is 10% on your current earnings, you might decide to save 3% and spend 7% in order to improve your lifestyle. You could tweak this to 4% and 6% too if you are already living at a level that you are happy with.

   This is an excellent way to commit to and save additional amounts without feeling a pinch since it comes from income that is going to be incremental from your current levels.

   It might sound like a small thing, but if you calculate this, done just three times in the next 10 years can mean an increased contribution of 19% to the Happiness Fund.

4. *Living Home and Owned Assets.* For many of us, especially in India, a living home is an emotion more than an asset or investment. It is a basic security that we aspire for. If you own a Home and have no mortgage for it, excluding the opportunity cost from your Financial Freedom Statement, might help you to bring down the targets too.

   I prefer to count the opportunity cost in because it works as a buffer for any unforeseen events during this entire plan period. These opportunity costs can help you absorb those!

5. *Enough Shock Absorbers.* At every stage of this chapter, with calculations and paradigms, and now the plan range we are attempting to build in shock absorbers everywhere. Shocks will come, unexpected market crashes and personal events and inflation and many other things can impact and affect the stability of your plan.

   The interest range taken to be conservative at Financial Levels [6%], the Opportunity Costs Built in, the Leverage planned with the 3 paradigms and connecting your savings plan to your incremental income, are all ways to have buffer systems at each stage.

   Above everything, remember each time one door closes, another one certainly has opened for you.

   You are now set to try out different combinations to see what is more achievable for you. You might want to tabulate what the scenario would be if you have consistent 6% Compound Returns for 20 years viz-a-viz a 9-10% for a period of 8 years.

   You might finally decide on an investment allocation which is distributed between the two ends, or a complete midway path. This is what the stalwarts call "Asset Allocation" in the technical jargon!

   This chapter is not about a list of places to invest in. That can change by the time you read this book the nth time and would thus, not be appropriate to put into a book. But it is indicative enough for you to understand what your financial goals are, and what the paradigms are and build a plan that is personalized for you.

Investments can broadly be divided into two kinds. Those that are targeted to fund your Financial Security Level, which you want for protection, basic needs and a security you can't compromise with. The other bucket is where growth can happen. It holds the potential for exponential growth, and if played and managed well, you can create wealth out of this bucket. Although, it comes with its risks.

Understanding these buckets and using this system to plan your Money Management System ensures you always have a balanced portfolio to get to your financial goals.

Investment Buckets and Suggested Asset Categories

A behavioural study found that when one apple was given to a monkey, he was very happy. When the second apple was given, he was ecstatic.

Then, the second apple was taken away. He was frustrated. So frustrated that he didn't enjoy the first apple that was still with him!

This is typical human behaviour. What we have and then lose can create havoc in our minds. The plan and strategy are on paper, but the real impacts of financial goals are not only on our numbers but also on our minds. Preservation is as important as generation of wealth.

We essentially have two buckets as per two of the possible risk profiles.

{Security Bucket}

As the name suggests, this bucket is linked to your Financial Security Level. Your Living home, utilities, the amount to put food on the table, to get from place to place, to keep you warm, safe and secure. Insurance, Medical and Emergency Fund. Basically, this relates to the investments you make keeping in mind the security levels that you can't play with.

This is the invested amount that you can't afford to lose. So, you can't afford to risk. In this bucket, you must focus on putting aside amounts and the related returns that will be available whenever you need them.

It is like your safety net. You lock up the funds in here and don't rethink or look back on them. Let them grow, slowly but steadily. The high-security fixed returns assets are usually on the lower end of the spectrum. About 6% on current levels.

This is the boring bucket. Not something you would even want to talk about. It is the slow parallel which fails to offer you the thrill of the fast ride, of pulsating returns and growth and the sexy exponential bit. It's not rock and roll but it gives you the comfortable joy of relaxed soul music, that you can dip into whenever you need relief.

- **Cash or Cash Equivalents**

  Cash in its most liquid form is the easiest and fastest to use when required in a short span of time. Many individuals have assets and thus, their net worth is substantial, but their liquidity may be crunched if they do not have enough assets that can bring them quick liquidity.

  It's a good idea to have some cash on you in your proximity. Like they say "under the mattress" or in Indian households, in the *dabbas* of grocery!

  Cash in a bank's Savings Account which gives you a low rate of interest is also a good idea since the auto sweep facility in recent years ensures that you have immediate access to funds in these accounts and also the benefit of earning interest on the same.

  The digital payment methods and any time withdrawal systems make money kept in the bank almost as liquid and usable as cash.

  For a regular savings account, the interest rate is about 4-5% with some banks offering as much as 6% in India.

  Kept in cash at home, of course, yields no interest, but is the safest method to have any time liquidity.

- **Fixed Term Deposits**

  Term Deposits or fixed Deposits in India were a consistent source of income for the middle-class and was popular with senior citizens. Once at 12%, in the recent years, the rate of interest has dropped to 6% in most cases. Some banks offer better interest for Senior Citizens [above the age of 60 years] going up to 7.50%.

Some NBFCs [Non-Banking Finance Companies] offer a higher rate as well. There are many which have a good reputation and track record. It is advisable to research these and see their performance before you invest. Although they may be renowned companies, we must take into account that being NBFCs they do not have a Banking License and thus, do not fall under the systems set by the Central Bank of the Country.

- **Bonds**

Bonds are fixed return instruments which also often come with Tax Saving options built in. With barely any risk, Bonds come with lower returns as compared to aggressive investments.

Bonds come with a fixed return rate and fixed tenure. The Income Tax Act also allows exemptions in certain cases for prescribed investments. One popular Tax Saving provision is for Long Term Capital Gains. The gains invested in specified Bonds make the amount tax exempt.

Usually, the returns on Bonds are around 5% but there are a few which can give a yield of 6% too.

Bonds can be purchased online through trading platforms through a bid and held in your Demat account. Government Bonds are one of the safest investments in India due to their Sovereign Guarantee and can be purchased through Stock Brokers too.

- **Home**

Your Living Home is not only an asset but has more sanctity attached to it. Although it is an asset which you can monetize if you decide to, it is a good idea to exclude your living home from the calculations when planning your financial goals. Although your home might be one of the highest valued assets in your books from a money standpoint, monetizing it might not be the best thing to do.

As a living home, it is a certain entry into the security bucket despite being an illiquid asset.

Real Estate other than your living home can be an interesting asset class to enter. Once upon a time, it was the most prominent asset class for the upper-middle-class and rising Indians. But this is more appropriate to be classified under the Growth-Risk Bucket.

- **Life Insurance**

Term Insurance is a life insurance product that offers life coverage to the insured. Opting for this ensures that your family and dependents get the insured amount after your death. This is more pertinent if you are the sole or main earning member and if your sudden absence can cause a Financial Disruption for those you leave behind.

An *Endowment Plan* is a life insurance product that along with insurance, includes an investment component. In this case, you have a dual advantage. If you survive beyond the term of the policy, you get the invested amount with the returns. In case of your death during the policy, your nominees get the amount.

The premium in the case of the term insurance is lower since it is only correlated to the eventuality of death during the policy tenure. The Endowment Policy accounts for the fact that it is more of an investment scheme with a life cover. So, the payout in either of the two cases is certain for the Insurance Company. Thus, the premium for this is much higher.

- **PPF**

Public Provident Fund [PPF] is an open-to-all investment that you can make through select banks and *India Post*. The amount that you invest in PPF works with the advantage of the compound interest returns. The longer you stay invested the more the cumulative returns.

The entire lump sum can be withdrawn at the end of the period. Usually, PPF works for 15-year tenures but can be renewed any number of times. Currently, the interest rate is 7.1% per annum compounded annually.

{Risk ~ Growth Bucket}

This is the bucket that is your 'upward push' bucket. It's where the growth and the fun and the rock and roll really lies. It's where exponential jumps and the rags-to-riches stories are waiting to happen.

It is also the place where you would have to be prepared to lose a part or even the full of what you invest. Of course, you will study all you can, balance your risks and take the right advice. But this is the aggressive and floating returns kind of asset bracket.

This is where you can see surges of quick growth but also have to be prepared for the dips that emerge. The goal is to always keep this bucket balanced and without having the pressure of time and context. Which means, if you are invested in this bucket and the returns are on a downward swing, you must have the holding capacity to let it stay until the recovery happens, and until it's a good idea to exit.

I repeatedly have been reminding you to keep emotions out of money! And in this bucket, the other keyword is 'patience.' The patience to hold on when everyone is exiting out of fear. A good asset will bounce back like we all do; you only have to give it time. So clearly, this is not where you can put funds that you might need access to without notice.

- **Equity**

  Stocks and Shares are probably the most popular investment options which are also known as quick vehicles for exponential growth.

The investments in this asset class have a much higher rate of returns if managed well, but also have a higher risk attached. As we all know, markets have their own movement and their own economy. It is impossible to accurately predict these movements even for stalwarts. But with the right education and experience, one can average out returns and get it right most of the time.

For any asset class in the Growth-Risk Bucket, the question to ask yourself is can you afford to risk this amount? If you can't remove it at your will or if you lose it altogether.

I suggest allocating 5% of your total wealth for this asset class. The amount you can play with, afford to hold, delay the use of, and even lose in a worst-case scenario.

- **Real Estate**

  Properties were popular and high-yield assets for decades, especially in the Indian context due to constant appreciation in property prices.

  Investing in a property with a view to renting it out, added to the appreciation that happens on the side, is still a lucrative investment. Cities and towns that are still developing usually can give a larger appreciation due to a fairly lower entry price and thus, more of a margin. It also becomes easier in this way to invest in different smaller and low-priced properties than to put everything into a high-ticketed one.

Short-term trade on properties is also common if you have high liquidity. Investing in under-construction or just about to be completed properties and exiting them within a few months can sometimes yield jackpot results.

However, for all real estate deals, the tax angle is pertinent. Short Term Capital gains is taxed at regular rates, tax benefits become available for a property if you hold it for a minimum of three years. The cost-benefit analysis is important to make sure the gains are not eaten away by the taxes.

- **High Yield Bonds**

The High Yield Bonds are the lower Security and Higher Returns version of the Bonds in the Security Bucket. There are several Bond options open for investment where the returns are higher, but the tax and the risks related are also higher than the Government Issued Bonds.

- **Collectables**

Artefacts, Art, Antiques, Wines, Coins, Statues. These are the collectable possessions that you would usually buy out of a passion or interest and perhaps, not look at it from the "Returns" point of view. Although they can be resold at premium prices and sometimes the returns can be manifold, it is a high-risk investment for two reasons. The demand for these comes from the connoisseurs and so it can be sparse. Secondly, since the Acquisition Cost for this is more negotiation based, factoring in the probable returns as a part of your financial planning can be a challenge.

- **Commodities**

  This class includes Gold, Silver, Coffee, Cotton, Oil and so on. Gold at one time used to be an asset that people would put their money into. It was considered a long-term asset which one could wear as ornaments, store and preserve as coins or bars, and it had both the concept of liquidity when one needed, and also didn't have the risk of value drop since gold traditionally had been on a rise through the decades.

  The commodity market is a structured market controlled through an exchange where commodities get traded. Akin to the stock market. Most Trading and Demat accounts enable you to buy and sell stocks and commodities both.

{Dream Bucket}

This is that Extra Bucket! The 'extra' ordinary, the 'extra' luxury, the 'extra'vagance!

This is the bucket that drives you. After all the study, planning and building your Money Management System, what is it all worth if you don't, along the way, enjoy some of the things that define *Fun, Fulfilment and Happiness*?

This is the bucket you can really put all your dreams into. The amounts we would need to fulfil those things that really matter. After all, the fun is not only the destination. It is more often in the journey! You don't want to miss all the fun and spends you can enjoy today in the bid to save for tomorrow!

The Three ways to Fill this Bucket

1. If you have a Bonus Win from anywhere. An Increment, a Windfall, any gain out of the blue, you can decide to divide this and put it into all the buckets. Ideally, you may go for three equal parts. So, if your gain is INR 30,000 you can put 10,000 into all three buckets adding to this pool.
2. When you have a phenomenal gain in the Growth-Risk Bucket, a jackpot gain, you can put it straight into the Dream Bucket or split it in two between security and dreams!
3. If you are a believer in more of a consistent discipline, then you can also opt to set aside a part of your income every month into the dream bucket. Remember this is over and above what you set aside for the other two and you are not allowed to touch anything out of the Security Bucket for your Dreams!

This has been a lot of work, I know. But you are better equipped now. You know what exactly you need in your Happiness Fund to build the various financial goals you have. To live the life that you desire for yourself and your loved ones.

You also know your options on how you can consistently increase your disposable capital and find the set-off between the time in hand and the returns on investment to align and re-align the balance in your favour.

You now understand what asset classes come under each of these categories of risk and safety, and what options you might want to choose from when you build your personalised plan.

We are living in a volatile world and things change quickly. There may be more options coming up from time to time. You can stay connected with me and my team through our various channels of connection to receive updates and newer, powerful ideas from time to time.

As I like to conclude most of my emails,

Here's wishing you abundance along the way as you begin this journey to achieving complete financial freedom!

Chapter 3.7
The Complete Transformation Toolkit for the Left-Brained

This part of the book, the last few chapters, have been all about the practical work you can do to find some basic information about your own money position and to raise the bar for yourself. The various chapters here are meant for you to work with as many times as you want to tweak or adjust the numbers and attune your mind to taking quicker and more informed decisions in relation to your financial goals.

Time and again, on the right brain work, you would need the Support Toolkit to keep working on your mindset and letting money into your life by constantly clearing anything that blocks it. Similarly, for the left-brain work, there are several techniques and tools I have used and people I have worked with have used in order to see a 180-degree change in their financial and life situations.

Most processes are in the earlier chapters. This is an extra list of tools you can use to get clarity, tweak your goals, set and reset your path and upskill yourself. Come back to this chapter and pick whatever resonates with you to do it repeatedly.

1. {180 Days ~ Muscle Memory}

- Any new technique needs practice, and then, the discipline to continue with that practice repeatedly until it gets wired into your system.
- Do you remember the first time you got in the driving seat of a car? The instructor tells you how to use the accelerator, brake and clutch. The eye coordination to keep a watch on the rearview and side view mirrors while you simultaneously release the clutch and take the accelerator. Once the car gets into motion you leave the clutch completely. It all sounded like too much to do all at once. You fumbled, you left the clutch too early or too late and the car jumped. But you kept doing it. Now, when you drive the car, you don't even need to think about all this. It is wired. You can do everything at once, speed up, listen to music or eat or drink, and freely talk to people in the car with you. This is the power of practice, of wiring, of making something an ingrained habit.
- Once you have found what it is that you want to set your goals for, you also know the discipline you need to create in order to get there. But until you don't practice that frequently, you are not going to be wired with it. When you are learning something new, upskilling or forming new habits, be sure to work out a plan so that you can do it for 90 days at a stretch! 90 days do it as part of your commitment, and another 90 to wire it in.

- Psychologists say that anything done for 180 days can be wired into the system. We can do it almost automatically and the effort that we have to put into it goes down considerably. Want to lose weight? Want to save money? Want to start investing? Want to start your day early? All you need is to dedicate yourself to the daily routine commitment for 180 days! Every single day.

2. {You First}

- One of the mistakes you will catch yourself making often. Doing business? And you don't pay yourself a salary. In a job and you don't keep aside anything for yourself.
- Starting right now, fix an amount that is for you each month. If it's a business, then declare a salary you will now pay yourself. If it's a job, decide how much you will put aside for yourself with each month's salary.
- This is not for any of the buckets, it is not a saving or investment. It is an amount for you. To spend, save or do whatever with.

3. {10% Principle}

- Access talks of this principle. Most financial and business coaches too. But access talks of this in a different way.
- Whatever comes to you, in cash or in your bank account, immediately remove 10% of it aside. To a separate account or in cash. Stash it away.

- This 10% doesn't go into any system, not into any bucket. It is not only from your income but anything that you receive.
- The 10% always with you keeps you grateful and feeling secure. The knowledge of always having an amount kept aside gives a subtle subconscious comfort. Try it and believe it for yourself!

4. {Bucket Paradigm}

Refer to chapter titled your Personalised Money Management System.

5. {Your Obituary}

- Do this exercise when you have time on hand. Preferably by yourself.
- Write your obituary as you would like it to appear.
- Get specific about what should be written about you. Make it an obituary feature and not a classified! Get into the details.
- Read it when done. Which of these are already on your goals? Which are those you are already working towards? Are there skills you want to learn, relationships you want to mend, or stories you want to change in order to get there?
- Tear the paper and discard it. If you want to do the process again in future, start over from scratch.

6. {Upskilling}

- List out three new skills you want to learn. They don't have to be those that will make you earn more money. They can be skills you always wanted to learn and didn't. Like a language or a musical instrument. Or maybe cycling if you don't know how to. Anything at all.
- Put a number against each. This number indicates the number of months in which you will start learning this. Today, everything can be learnt virtually too. Costs also are not prohibitive anymore with options opening up endlessly. So, no excuses!
- Take the first step now. Get information, sign up for their newsletter. Leave your interest form. Talk to someone who has done this before to chat about it. Do one thing; take one step towards it.

7. {Practice Asking}

- Asking the right questions will bring you the right answers. The context of the questions often determines the answers you will get in return.
- Two Monks were strolling in the garden by the monastery one day. Monk 1 asked Monk 2, "How come you are listening to music when walking in nature? Have you asked the Master?"

  Monk 2 replied, "Yes, indeed, the Master gave me permission."

Monk 1 asks again, "How can that be? I asked the Master and he said no!"

Monk 2 asks "What did you ask Him?"

Monk 1 replies "Can I listen to music when I do open-eye meditation in the garden? I asked the Master this and He said No. What did you ask?"

Monk 2 says, "I asked if it is alright for me to do open-eye meditation when I am listening to music in the garden. He said, 'yes.'"

If you are looking for answers, practice asking the right questions!

As we come to the end of the book, remember this is not the end but a beginning. Should you ever need to connect with me for anything, you can find me or my team on any media.

I Wish you Luck! I wish you the perseverance and the grit to go all out and get what you want and so deserve, to live the life of your dreams!

To shine bright and let the world see the magic that is you!

4.
Conclusion

Chapter 4.0

Real Life Stories/Case Studies

Stories can be compelling agents of change. Real Stories, anecdotes and case studies can offer us both comfort and inspiration on difficult days. I think life is a series of problem-solving and challenge resolution situations. Your ability to solve problems and face them head-on might be the catalyst to a new reality.

I have picked three stories with different challenges and equally different resolutions. The one takeaway I want you to have from these is to know that *every challenge has a resolution; every problem brings with it the solution.*

1. **Punjab Based Private Limited Pharma Company [Family Owned]**

The Challenge

A pharma company that was started out of a small *Kothi* (old styled cottage in northern India) in a district of Punjab in 1919, flourished and became a pharma leader by the mid-1990s. Their third generation is now handling the company.

Originally an HUF, with the business rights given to only the male heirs, the two brothers who are handling the business currently are running parallel departments in the company. Amanpreet and Harpreet (name changed) are both great at what they lead.

Amanpreet is the front-ender, the speaker, the deal-clincher. Harpreet is the person on the backend. Ideation, strategy and the best ideas for production and innovation come from him.

The company has seen a sharp rise in its year-on-year growth consistently for the last 15 years. But in the last 2 years, there was a strange phenomenon that started showing up.

Although the revenues were seeing the same rate of accelerating growth, the profits were moving in a decelerating manner. Which meant, if left unattended, the profits would be eroded soon and would turn into losses.

During the weeks that followed, we delved deeper into the systems, books of accounts and all internal communication trails. Nothing was found. The audits were effective, the cost of production was in check, sales hadn't seen a dip and, in fact, were on a rise at a consistent rate. There was nothing visible to the eye that was the cause of the uncontrollable operating costs that were rising in the books.

We picked up all the high-value transactions and brought out the trail for each of these. Incidentally, we found a pattern in them. Whenever there was an allocation made by any one director, it was closely followed by the other. Budgets were suddenly increased for different pre-determined and provided-for expenses which didn't make logical sense.

For instance, the increase in business Development Budget was requested by the concerned department and approved by Amanpreet, which had pushed the operating costs by a whopping 21%. Soon after was another transaction where Harpreet had sanctioned a series of business workshops and welfare schemes for their entire workforce for upskilling, which had pushed up the operating costs by another 22%. Patterns showed both ways.

Two things were clear. The decisions were running neck to neck; they were clearly out of a 'one upmanship' in the company – decisions made out of emotion rather than business prudence.

And we know by now, emotions have to be kept out of money decisions!

How it was Resolved

We had a one-to-one chat with the Human Resource Head and understood the dynamics between the board members. The autocratic way of working that had crept in due to lack of mutual trust was already creating conflicts and it was certain to take the company down if this was not stopped.

We built a new system of change.

1. *Amanpreet and Harpreet would now sanction budgets for each other's departments. Which meant for every request in upward revision of budgeting, all front ending departments that came under Amanpreet had to table their proposal to Harpreet and vice versa.*

2. *A New Board Resolution made the budget revisions permissible only once a quarter and to be conducted as part of a mandatory review of all departments. This ensured that concurrent department reviews and budget submissions had to be completed in a closed tender style. All requests were opened at once. There was no way for people to get time to let their egos play.*

3. *The last was the real solution. We moderated communication sessions between the two directors for a period of 12 weeks, once every week. During this time, we made the sessions fun, brought out common interests and did one offsite activity. Both of them love live music and good food. So, we arranged for a group outing. We also encouraged their mother to help them communicate more openly on the home front, in their personal space.*

Lessons

Lack of communication and resulting ego hassles were causing an energy shift. This was seeping into the business decisions they were making. Opening up, having fun and communicating openly had brought them to realise that the differences were only perceived. Points 1 and 2 helped in handholding them to a certain level of discipline until they had worked through the process.

Point 3 made them realise that they could do much better as a team than by working against each other. Working as a team would be great for business and at home. Reduced friction would mean better head space, increased productivity and clearer decision making. In the following 12 months, the business had a complete turnaround.

2. Sudden Death of a Young Founder

The Challenge

This AI-backed tech setup was started by this IIM-IIT Graduate from Raipur, India. It's what 'small-town big dreams' are made of. Planned right, thought out right and done right.

He got his mother on the company board since he didn't have a co-founder yet, until he could find one. The start-up was doing well, generating revenue and inching closer to profit generation.

Covid 19, which snuffed out a lot of bright lights, hit out of the blue. Stuck in the midst of a work trip and forced to come in contact with people he couldn't trace contacts for, Amit (name changed) died of multiple organ failure in June 2020.

Having lost his father early, he left behind a grieving mother and a younger sister, all of 17. One would think this would be the start of the end. His mother had been a teacher earlier in her career and was now a homemaker for a long time. His sister was still studying. The company had no debt, but it did have two small investors.

When my team got in touch with his mother and sister, since they were his legal heirs, they were both not in the headspace to even give it a thought. For the next 8 months, we kept the investors in the loop. His core team involved was really good and kept the company afloat. His shares were transferred to the sister. His mother was already a shareholder. We inducted one of the investors as a second director.

Although the soul of the company was gone, the investors and the core team were doing a great job to create growth metrics that could take the start-up to the next level.

One year after Amit's passing, we moderated a final discussion between the investors and his family. No paradigms really were working for the family. Neither passion nor skills and surely, it wasn't going to be a lucrative idea *for them* to run it.

If they had any reservations about quitting the company and selling their shares out to the others, it was the emotion. It was Amit's dream. And it was like abandoning his dream. But you know now that we keep emotions out of money decisions! And yet, we can't let go off some emotions fully. So, a little is permitted!

How it was Resolved

The investors along with the core team were doing a great job. The 3-paradigm rule fitted perfectly with them as a team.

1. *The shares that belonged to Amit, which were now with his sister, were 49%. The original shares with both Investors combined were 10%. The remaining 41% were with Amit's mother. The investors agreed to get the shares valued with a 7-year*

projection. The value of the company was working out 10 times from where this had all begun a few years ago.

2. *Out of the 41% stakes with Amit's mother, 31% were bought over by new incoming investors, with an ESOPs* (Employee Stock Options Plan) *option given to the core team members from the new reshuffled share-holding position.*

3. *Out of the 49% the existing investors bought 44%. Now, the new shareholding ratio was: Amit's family 15%, Investors total 85%.*

4. *15% of the shares remained with Amit's family. This took care of their emotional view and also kept them participating in the future profits of the company when it grew.*

5. *At the current 10X valuation, the family also got a large amount of liquidity for their 75% dilution.*

6. *The core team became stakeholders and the investors – now the company owners – could work on creating the story which was once Amit's dream.*

Lessons

Although money decisions can't be taken in an emotional state, it is alright to once in a while, take emotions into consideration when you are problem-solving in business. It is also completely alright to let go of an "opportunity" if that is not what resonates with you, like what Amit's family did. It would have been easy for them to get carried away with the idea of keeping his dream alive, even if it was not what they really wanted to or could do. With this mature decision, they could keep his dream alive more effectively by letting those who could take it to new heights do that.

3. 53-Year-Old Founder, High Revenues but no Cash in Hand at the end of the Month.

The Challenge

Early retirement from a corporate position, a golden handshake as it was called 15 years ago and the desire to do something on his own! The story is not new. Many individuals who do exceedingly well in their jobs often find themselves stuck when they decide to enter the enticing world of business.

I use the word 'enticing' on purpose.

The business and entrepreneurship world fascinates many. If there was one single myth that has taken more businesses down than anything else, it has got to be the idea that 'you can do business if you have the capital!' There is no truth farther than that.

Vithal's (name changed) journey began after his early retirement. He had 20+ years of experience in a position that he had excelled in to climb the ladder quickly. He wasn't a premium institute graduate, but he was an intelligent implementor and a quick learner in his field. Looking back, his journey from his moderate beginnings until this point was incredible.

Equipped with the funds, his passion to make it big on his own and the support of his family, he rolled up his sleeves to start his venture! He invested a great deal of money (close to 28 Lacs!), hired a capable team, created his asset block and began production.

His venture was to manufacture spare parts for mid-sized vehicles. Having been in the automobile industry for 20 years, Vithal knew the industry – procurement, quality control measures, managing blue-collar employees, supplier networks and sales strategy. He was well connected with the dealer networks and automobile companies to find a market.

In less than 22 months, the business began to show great traction. The sales were picking up, production quality was getting talked about, repeat customers, large contracts; everything was falling in place.

As the financial year came to an end and he sat with his accountant to take stock of the performance, what came to light was shocking. Despite the sales figures, the teamwork, great product quality and his dedication to making the venture work, the cash and bank balances were dismal. Upon going a bit deeper, they both realized the situation was actually cash-crunched.

There wasn't enough to pay the taxes for the year and all the operating costs that month. There were pending supplier payments too.

What had actually happened? Remember in the beginning when we discussed why so many businesses fail, we talked about the phenomenon of cash flow management. The lack of money management skills. Driving that point home. Sales were good, so money was coming in. But the "how to use that money to the optimum level" part – that skill was clearly lacking.

Vithal wasn't even drawing a salary. He was managing his home expenses from his savings, which also were beginning to dry up. He had a debt which he had taken to supplement the initial setup, which was piling up too. So, basically, everything was as bad as it could possibly get. Now, there was only one way left, the way up!

How it was Resolved

Different accounts for different expense heads of the business to be allocated daily without thought or decision making brought in the way. Periodic stock taking. Daily Sheets. Credit and Payment timelines. Auto Debits for most important and time-bound payments.

1. *Four new bank accounts were set up in four different banks with online transfer and net-banking facilities. One account was designated for receiving all sales happening through credit cards, digital payment methods, etc. Any Cash collections were also to be deposited in the same designated account. This was the account where every sale transaction to the last rupee was put. Let's call this the primary account.*

2. *Four Transfers were made every day out of the daily sales amounts.* Yes, every single day. Who said discipline is easy!

    30% towards fixed operating costs,

    12% towards taxes,

    10% towards payment to the founder.

    The last 10% as reserves or profit.

And the balance of 38% remained in the primary account.

3. *The primary account had the remainder 38% to be utilised for all the payments and procurements. The reserve was a back-up which was available in case the procurement and daily spends required a little more. The idea was to eventually practice this system and learn to manage the procurements within this 38%. Then, the reserve could be profit directly.*

4. *Stock was to be taken every week and sent to our team who was helping Vithal's team learn new processes. New supplier contracts were drawn up with a fixed rate pricing, since everything was bulk buying.*

5. *The pricing strategy was re-planned. Standard costing was worked out (for the first ever time) and the selling price was fixed with a cost-plus-margin method.*

6. *At the end of the first month of this exercise, for the first time, Vithal had all his expenses and payments sitting in different accounts. The primary account had got exhausted and he also had to dip into the reserves account for another 4%. But all operating costs were paid on time, taxes paid up; for the first time, he took a salary home and he still had a reserve amount of 6% which was his profit!*

Lessons

Turning losses into profits might sometimes be only a matter of discipline and having the right methods and systems to follow. The ideal way is for founders to take the time and energy to take some basic money management training so that they can keep this discipline in the long run.

But like in the case of Vithal, who just didn't want to do that, the next best way is to set up a system and train the teams to carry out every decided function without any drops in the process flow. He had no inclination to get involved and take charge of the financial discipline. So, he opted for the second option.

A great system put in place and adhered to with discipline can bring about the same results.

Stories are all around us. If you make it a habit to be observant and watch the lives of those around you, it is an easy task to be able to start understanding the correlation between what people do and what the results are. This becomes easier when they are people you might not personally know and so, can have a more unbiased or objective view about.

Through this entire book, what we have worked on is to build both the resilience and the awareness to what the ingredients of a dream life are.

Choose someone you can observe closely, someone's life you find closest to the life of your dreams. Watch what they have done and what they are doing.

How do they relate to the people around them?

What kind of relationships do they have with their closest circle of five?

What workouts are they doing and what do their daily meals look like?

Observe what they read and what music they listen to. Their social calendar. The hobbies they pursue. Their workout schedule.

I am not asking you to emulate what they do. But if they are the hero you want to be like, be sure you get the right reasons for choosing them as your hero.

More importantly, be sure what has gone into becoming them. This can be a good way to understand how the principles play out and to add what resonates with you into your life plan!

Chapter 4.1

Frequently Asked Questions

1. Does manifestation really work? Have you seen it happen?

Yes. I have seen it happen. Several times. I am an accidental millionaire because someone else is an intentional one! When we had first moved into our own home, for the first few years, our budgets remained tight and things difficult. One such year, the Ganesh Utsav was round the corner and my dad looked worried because he still had a lot of payments to come through that were getting delayed. The Ganesh Utsav which we had started celebrating in 1984 itself, at home, was one time of the year that we would save up for and do it in the best possible way. This year looked like a challenge. When he mentioned this to my mom, she said she didn't want to compromise on it and so he needn't worry and she would take care of it.

With the marriage, then abuse, the time out during her repeated pregnancies and then wanting to put her focus on motherhood, mom wasn't actively pursuing a career anymore. So, when she said this, I don't think any of us (including her) knew what she meant or how it was going to happen.

3 days later, she decided she would put up one of her artworks for sale. It was a work of Krishna Arjun [depiction of the Gita Updesh ~ the time when Krishna gave the Gita to Arjun on the battlefield]. This was etched metal work which was a new blossoming art in those days.

*Although her regular medium was oil paints on canvas, she had learnt this art only recently and this was her first big work in etched metal. It was large (perhaps 3 ft * 8 ft.)*

{In case I have missed telling you, my mom was a graduate in fine arts, and painting remained her first love!}

She spoke to a few people she was in touch with from her Jehangir Art Gallery days [for the unversed, this gallery is both where art shows happen and where some of the best artists also spend a lot of their time]. It used to house a café called Samovar for decades, which was a go-to place for the new brewing artists in the 1960s and 70s, I am told. Unfortunately, this café shut doors in 2015 after running for more than five decades.

One of her friends from there connected mom to an agent [for the want of a better word!] who was procuring art for one of his clients.

He came home and saw the work (no mobile phones, no instant cameras, no digital messaging and no smartphones, remember!)

It was 6 days from the time she had said she would manage the Ganesh Utsav this time. The Gitopdesh [the title she had given it] got sold for Rs. 1.50 lacs! For middle-class homes in the 1980s, this amount was more than a month's earnings! The current value of this amount indexed at inflation rates from 1987 to 2022, would be 17.59 lacs!

This is a small instance. She manifested our first home. She manifested horses! Her childhood dream of owning one, translated into a small farm a couple of hours from home.

I think, she also manifested me!

2. **According to you, Money Management Skills are what makes Business and Life work. Can this skill be acquired by people with no background in Finance?**

Of course, it can be. Although I know an entire book written on the subject might make you feel it is a difficult thing to achieve. But really, money skills are simple. It is not rocket science.

You know who the best money managers in the world are?

Homemakers! I mean, look at them. They manage with the fixed amount given to them. They know exactly how to use the bucket systems. They learn how to optimize every spend, and so, they probably have the highest awareness of the opportunity cost concept.

They inherently set monthly goals and remain agile to reach them. They are excellent team managers and leaders. They're good decision makers.

Look out for role models who didn't have a finance background around you. Observe how they do it. Money management can be simple. It is the idea of functioning from a space of broke. Being innovative. Being resilient. Being flexible. Not going by the book or theories. Keeping your eyes and ears open. Chunk it down, and get the right people to help you in this journey.

You don't need maths or accounting or any other skill to learn money management or to find complete Financial Freedom.

Confession- Despite being qualified in finance and being an accidental millionaire, my money management skills were truly in question. My entrepreneurial journey of last 20 years gave me the hands-on training and practice to come from where I was to where I am. I call it the journey from accident to intention!

3. **What are the five skills I can start working on to make sound money decisions and manage money better? I am not from a finance background.**

It's difficult to encapsulate five. It is going to be a life-long learning process. I am still learning. But I can share five areas you can start taking charge of to move towards managing your money better.

- ***Stop giving your Power away****. A parent, spouse, advisor, sibling, child, friend, business partner, or lover. Whoever. Keep your finances within your purview. Someone helping you is different. At all times, be aware of every little transaction that happens around your money, even if you think you* *are not great at it. The other side of the same coin. If you are unintentionally taking someone's power away, make sure to give it back to them. Encourage those around you to take charge of their money and decisions. Sometimes, being always ready to solve a problem for your loved ones might be more damaging for them than you realize.*

- ***Learn to Read the Fine Print.*** *Don't ever sign a contract without reading it. Don't ever sign anything without reading. Read. Take time. Ask questions. If you don't understand something, ask more questions.*
- ***The 2% Rule. Don't make Rushed Decisions.*** *The last seat left. The last unit of the product you like. Last two hours of the best price offer. Let it go. Pass the 'opportunity.' Don't get rushed into any decision if you are spending more than 2% of your monthly earnings in that decision. Take 24 hours to think whenever someone rushes you to decide immediately and pay. You might think it's crazy to leave a good offer. Just do it.*
- ***Follow Systems.*** *The best way to take the risks out of your decision-making is to put a system to it. This becomes a guiding map for you to make quick decisions based on the guidelines and rules that are set prior, taking the dependence on your money skills out of day-to-day decisions. You can do this both on the home front and at work.*
- ***Keep Notes.*** *Keep records of spends. At the end of each day, see how much you have spent towards*

what. The new online and digital space has made payments so easy that sometimes, we don't realise the quantum we are spending each day. Until money management becomes second nature to you, continue to track every amount that goes out. You will be able to spot patterns of the spends and start beginning to control them as per your priorities.

4. I am 70. I don't think there is anything I can do now. My business wound up with me having to file for bankruptcy. I wish I could redeem myself. Any suggestions?

Age is just a number. I know that sounds overused and worn out, but it remains true. If you make your age the most pertinent part of your current situation, it will be.

Define what redemption is to you. Building another business? Or simply knowing you can succeed at what you decide to do now?

Have you considered what you might have lost in terms of time and energy over the years?

A place you wanted to travel to, friends you were waiting to reconnect with, a hobby you left at school to focus on your career. There are so many parts of us that reside inside. Define your redemption threshold and then, work towards it.

Remember the confidence goals we spoke of? How do winners build a habit of setting small goals every day that they can achieve, adding to their confidence bit by bit. Start with confidence goals!

5. What according to you is the most important skill I need to learn in order to find complete financial freedom?

Any positive culmination in life (or even negative for that matter), doesn't come from one skill or one act. Everything I have written about in this book and everything you can lay your hands on in the outside world, give it your all. After all, you are aiming for a dream life.

Nothing is linear. Do everything. Work on everything simultaneously. But also, be sure to make space for slowdowns, accept failures and redirect, find ways to keep your confidence going, get clearer and better at goal setting. Learn new skills, get a hero, read or listen. It is easier than you think. But commitment is non-negotiable.

10 Books that Changed my Life... and could change yours

1. **Eat that Frog – Brian Tracy**
2. **Awaken the Giant Within – Tony Robbins**
3. **The Big Leap – Gay Hendricks**
4. **Get Rich Lucky Bitch – Denise Duffield Thomas**
5. **The Compound Effect – Darren Hardy**
6. **Cash Quadrants – Robert Kiyosaki**
7. **God Loves Fun – Sri Sri Ravi Shankar**
8. **Blink – Malcolm Gladwell**
9. **Ikigai – Hector Garcia & Francesc Miralles**
10. **You can Heal your Life – Louis Hay**

We all have something to put on the table!

I have put what I know.

There are things I don't know yet. There are things I may never know.

Combined, we can transform the lives of millions. No one person holds the power to do that. Blockchain technology may be best used in knowledge and information that can transform lives.

If you have a story or an anecdote you would like to share, connect with me. If you think your story must find a voice and readers can learn from it, share it with me. I would love to hear it.

I wish you an abundant life, full of happiness, determination and the ability to translate your dream life into reality!

www.ingramcontent.com/pod-product-compliance
Lightning Source LLC
LaVergne TN
LVHW041148150826
845673LV00001B/97

9798887336893